CW01426327

Knocking Down The Wall

Muhammad Ali's Revolutionary Leadership for
Black America's Rise

by

DAVIS TRUMAN

Davis Truman© Copyright 2023 - All rights reserved.

The content contained within this book may not be reproduced, duplicated, or transmitted without direct written permission from the author or the publisher.

Under no circumstances will any blame or legal responsibility be held against the publisher, or author, for any damages, reparation, or monetary loss due to the information contained within this book. Either directly or indirectly.

Legal Notice:

This book is copyright protected. This book is only for personal use. You cannot amend, distribute, sell, use, quote, or paraphrase any part, or the content within this book, without the author's or publisher's consent.

Disclaimer Notice:

Please note the information contained within this document is for educational and entertainment purposes only. All effort has been executed to present accurate, up-to-date, and reliable, complete information. No warranties of any kind are declared or implied. Readers acknowledge that the author does not render legal, financial, medical, or professional advice. The content within this book has been derived from various sources. Please consult a licensed professional before attempting any techniques outlined in this book.

By reading this document, the reader agrees that under no circumstances is the author responsible for any losses, direct or indirect, which are incurred as a result of the use of the information contained within this document, including, but not limited to, — errors, omissions, or inaccuracies.

Table of Contents

CHAPTER ONE

INTRODUCTION

Muhammad Ali, a renowned figure in American sports history, stands among the most influential athletes. His impact echoes that of numerous African Americans who have tirelessly contributed to the progress of the black community, spanning from the time of Phillis Wheatley to the era of the civil rights movement, famously led by Martin Luther King, Jr. Without a doubt, Ali rightfully deserves a prominent position among esteemed black intellectuals. His nontraditional platform of sports served as a resounding voice of freedom for African Americans, and no other athlete embodied the movement more than Ali. It is fitting that a boxer spearheaded the endeavor of African American athletes in their quest for racial justice. Both inside and outside the ring, through his physical prowess and impassioned rhetoric, Ali captivated the global audience.

Ali had a remarkable oratory talent, evident in his love for conversation. Even as a relatively unknown eighteen-year-old during the 1960 Rome Olympics, his fellow Olympian Paula Jean Myers Pope noted that Ali was constantly preaching in the cafeteria, on the grounds, in the vast village, downtown, or at the boxing venue. His words naturally drew people towards him. Recognized alongside the world's esteemed figures, British writer Richard Harris fervently stated that Ali stands shoulder-to-shoulder with Mandela, one of the globe's great heroes, prompting introspection on the reasons behind this parallel. How and why did Ali ascend to such global prominence? These essential inquiries define Ali's legacy. In essence, Ali's undeniable eminence over the past sixty years complemented the efforts of earlier leaders like Frederick Douglass, W.E.B. DuBois, and Martin Luther King, Jr. The profound impact of his words on a global scale perplexes even Pulitzer Prize-winning author David Remnick, who marvels at how a lanky youth from segregated Louisville transformed himself into one of the greatest improvisers in American history, a figure akin to Davy Crockett, Walt Whitman, and Duke Ellington. Clearly, Ali's rhetoric and actions added significant weight to the pursuit of equality, justifying his place in the intellectual continuum of African American advancement throughout American history.

Ali exhibited extraordinary talent as a boxer, showcasing his artistry within the ring while maintaining a keen awareness of his significance beyond the realm of sports. Hugh McIlvanney, a prominent British sportswriter with over six decades of experience, recognized Ali as an immensely exceptional human being, asserting that although sports provided his platform, his true stage was humanity. Embracing his humanitarian role, Ali consciously studied the contributions of influential African Americans who came before him and sought to build upon their legacies. His conduct defied the norms of segregation, making him a highly provocative figure. Barack Obama accurately remarked that Ali was a radical even during a time of radicalism, representing a resounding, proud, and unapologetically black voice in a Jim Crow society. While familiarizing himself with his predecessors, Ali also dedicated himself to understanding the various groups in the 1960s that actively resisted segregation. In a 1964 interview, he expressed his desire to educate himself on these matters:

> *I don't know who that Muslim speaker was, but everything he said made sense. The man made me think about many things I had wondered about. But I didn't join right away. I went to CORE, Urban League, and N.A.A.C.P. meetings. I studied the Catholics, the Jehovah's Witnesses, Seventh-day Adventists, Baptists, and Methodists in search of knowledge. The most concrete thing I found in churches was segregation. Well, now I have learned to accept my own and be myself. I know we are original men and that we are the greatest people on the planet Earth and our women the queens thereof.*

Ali's quest for knowledge stemmed from his experiences and interactions, profoundly shaped by his upbringing in Louisville within the confines of the Jim Crow South. Drawing from his family history, struggles, travels, and comprehensive understanding of the black experience, he became a conduit for the voices that preceded him. Years later, Ali reflected on the necessity of proving that a new kind of black man could exist, which required showcasing this to the world. His goal was to stand up against oppressors and dignify his race for the benefit of future generations. Despite graduating from Louisville's Central High School with a low rank and a perceived below-average IQ, Ali possessed a distinct brilliance.

Nonetheless, it was evident that he possessed a remarkable mind, as affirmed by his high school principal Atwood Wilson, who expressed to the faculty that their greatest claim to fame would be their association with Cassius Clay. Despite his academic shortcomings, Ali frequently served as a college graduation speaker, illustrating his mindfulness of history and innate ability to wield an unwavering and powerful voice in pursuing black advancement. Notably, even Martin Luther King, Jr. certainly acknowledged Ali's courage, regardless of one's opinions on his religion. Ali possessed the unique ability to transcend what preceded him, leaving an indelible impact on the progress of the black cause. Ali's medium of influence, or perhaps the medium that utilized him, derived from his position as the heavyweight champion, a platform his predecessors did not necessarily have access to. Ali emerged at an opportune moment when television was on the cusp of skyrocketing in popularity, fundamentally altering the dissemination of information worldwide. He recognized the example set by Jack Johnson, the first black heavyweight champion, who utilized his outspokenness in the early twentieth century. Ali adapted and refined this approach to suit the evolving landscape of the 1960s and 1970s, marked by the rapid growth of mass media and the constant presence of reporters and cameras.

With his mastery of language and captivating persona, Ali became an intriguing provocateur, attracting the attention of the press. Renowned British broadcaster Michael Parkinson once shared that when asked about the most remarkable person he had ever encountered, he unequivocally responded, "Ali. I interviewed him four times. I lost on every occasion." Ali simply mesmerized the public with his charisma and eloquence. At age twenty, he fearlessly declared his prediction of becoming the youngest heavyweight champion in history by the end of 1963. His self-assurance was unparalleled, making him an implausible figure, yet his words would soon resonate across the broadest circles.

While Douglass and DuBois can be regarded as "originators" of black thought, Ali served as a catalyst, advancing their cause through the available medium of his time. Ali took immense pride in his black identity, and his vocalization allowed other black individuals to live with a greater sense of dignity. Even in the face of persecution for defying the Vietnam War draft, he boldly expressed, "I'm so black, man, I don't care. I'm not going to compromise. I'm not going to do anything to mislead my people. I get pleasure out of walking down the alleys, walking through the ghettos, walking up to little black children." Ali wholeheartedly embraced the role of leading and setting an example for his black community, driven by a profound passion. For instance, he continued to fight well into the late 1970s, despite knowing the adverse effects on his health, because it provided him with an elevated platform to positively influence his followers. Ali became the embodiment and a source of inspiration for his race during a tumultuous era. Baseball legend Reggie Jackson candidly acknowledged the impact of

Ali's actions and words, speaking to their transformative effect:

Do you know what Ali meant to black people? He was the leader of a nation, the leader of black America. As a young black, at times, I was ashamed of my color; I was ashamed of my hair. And Ali made me proud. I'm just as happy being black now as somebody else is being white, and Ali was part of that growing process. I remember how I felt when Martin Luther King was assassinated. There was no one to cling to except Ali. I don't know what I would have done if I'd had that kind of leadership burden thrust upon me. . . . Do you understand what it did for black Americans to know that the most physically gifted, possibly the most handsome, and one of the most charismatic men in the world was black? Ali helped raise black people in this country out of mental slavery. The entire experience of being black changed for millions of people because of Ali.

Jackson's reference to mental slavery highlights the very essence of what Ali aimed to address. Having personally experienced the perils of prejudice in Louisville, Ali recognized the necessity of unwavering commitment to challenging deeply ingrained racism rooted in the dark days of slavery. He represented the complex tapestry of America's history, encompassing its shadows and light. Barack Obama candidly articulated this sentiment in his eulogy at Ali's funeral, stating, "Muhammad Ali was America. Brash, defiant, pioneering, joyful, never tired, always game to test the odds. He embodied our most fundamental freedoms, religion, speech, and spirit. He exemplified our capacity to reinvent ourselves. His life spoke to the original sin of slavery and discrimination, and his journey helped jolt our collective conscience and set us on a meandering path toward redemption. Like America, he was always a work in progress." Ali encountered numerous obstacles on his path toward redemption. Yet, one constant remained: his unwavering commitment to speak up and express his views on some of the most significant issues of his time. His defiance of societal norms was tangible and best encapsulated by one of the most profound statements of his life as he entered the global spotlight in 1964: "I know where I'm going, and I know the truth, and I don't have to be what you want me to be. I'm free to be what I want."

CHAPTER TWO

BLACK BOXING

The history of boxing intertwines with the African American experience, stretching back centuries to the sport's introduction to slaves from England. Slave owners exercised caution in allowing their slaves to engage in the brutal nature of boxing due to the fear of permanent injuries. They recognized the pivotal role that slaves played in their economic structures. Nevertheless, there were instances where southern plantation owners would match up slaves of seemingly equal strength and spectate as they fought, placing bets for their entertainment. These matches were often vicious, with slaves coming perilously close to death. It is no wonder that prominent abolitionists like Frederick Douglass abhorred boxing and wrestling, viewing them as exacerbating the wickedness inherent in the institution of slavery.

The establishment of the "color line" in boxing can be traced back to the actions of John L. Sullivan, the first champion of the modern era in the 1880s. Sullivan openly declared, "I will not fight a Negro. I never have, and I never shall." Jim Jeffries's successor made a similar vow and retired without facing a black opponent. However, Jeffries was compelled to break his promise when Jack Johnson emerged as the first black heavyweight champion of the world in 1908 after defeating Tommy Burns in Australia. Leading up to the fight against Burns, Johnson faced relentless racial harassment but remained focused and emerged victorious. This victory marked a significant moment for African Americans in sports. The New York Times summarized the fight's outcome the following day: "Johnson appeared fresh after the fight, while Burns' eyes were badly puffed and his mouth swollen to twice its normal size. The Canadian fought a game battle and showed indomitable pluck, but he was no match for the big black Texan." This event became a watershed moment in African-American history, as white society suddenly became fixated on seeking redemption.

Despite the displeasure of many American boxing fans, Johnson was awarded the championship and consistently defended it, fearlessly taking on all challengers. His demeanor and behavior often provoked and angered white individuals. After each fight, he would promptly take his earnings and indulge in extravagant purchases. Johnson deliberately scheduled fights against white opponents eager to reclaim their race's championship. He relished this antagonistic attitude, as he derived satisfaction from defeating angry white racists. The white establishment in America was desperate to find a suitable opponent for Johnson, and the press grew increasingly impatient with the situation.

Leading the charge in the press was Jack London, a renowned novelist and boxing correspondent for the New York Herald. London, who did not hold favorable views of the African-American community, published the now-famous lines in the Herald that caught the attention of Jeffries and compelled him to return to the ring: "Jeffries must emerge from his alfalfa farm and remove that smile from Johnson's face. Jeff, it's up to you." These words from London stirred up the former champion, pushing him out of retirement to answer the call for the "Great White Hope" and reclaim the heavyweight title for the Caucasian race. Jeffries, motivated by both his fans and racial biases, reluctantly agreed to return, stating, "I am going into this fight for the sole purpose of proving that a white man is better than a Negro." Jeffries' misguided motivation ultimately contributed to what would become the most famous sporting event of that time.

The fight was initially scheduled in San Francisco during the summer of 1910. Still, due to the influence of anti-boxing advocates, the governor of California refused to allow the "brutal exhibition" for moral reasons. As a result, the city of Reno eagerly stepped in to host the fight on the Fourth of July, hoping to gain recognition and notoriety. Under the training of former champion "Gentleman" Jim Corbett, Jeffries worked hard to shed weight and get into fighting shape for what was billed as the "Fight of the Century." The event proved immensely profitable for Reno's businesses, particularly the gambling casinos, and saloons. It was a momentous occasion that garnered worldwide attention, and according to Nevada historian Robert Laxalt, the population of

Reno more than doubled in the days leading up to the fight. He remarked, "Every hotel room in town was taken, and miles of special trains with sleeping cars lined the tracks."

On the day of the long-awaited fight, July 4, 1910, Johnson was met with cries of "Kill the nigger!" and "All Coons Look Alike to Me." The fans were crammed into the arena, custom-built for the occasion. The oppressive heat only contributed to the suspense of the bout since Johnson was clearly the superior fighter from the start. Johnson handled Jeffries with ease and tormented him from start to finish. In his memoirs, Johnson stated, "Hardly a blow had been struck when I knew that I was Jeff's master." Johnson knocked Jeffries out in the fifteenth round, and his corner forfeited the fight in the following round to avoid additional destruction. Laxalt said in his Nevada history, "Johnson battered the aging Jeffries into a helpless pulp." The audience was stunned and stunned. Surprisingly, there was no violence in Reno following the battle; but Reno did not represent the rest of the country. As blacks rejoiced over Johnson's win, some of the worst race riots in US history erupted nationwide. According to one Boston

American story, white Americans were evidently dissatisfied with the battle's outcome, "declaring that Independence Day had been dishonored and disguised by a brutal prize fight; that the moral sense of a nation had been outraged."

Riots were recorded in Arkansas, Colorado, Georgia, Illinois, Missouri, Nebraska, New York, Ohio, Pennsylvania, Texas, and Washington, D.C. Police saved a black man ready to be lynched in Manhattan. In contrast, a black man in Houston had his throat cut for celebrating Johnson's triumph. Thousands of whites gathered on Eighth Avenue, threatening to beat any black man who showed up, and author David Remnick claims that "no racial event since Martin Luther King Jr.'s assassination in 1968 would set off such a violent reaction." Ultimately, at least ten people were killed, and hundreds were injured. Racist whites followed Johnson everywhere he went, yelling, "Lynch him! Lynch him!" "Get rid of the nigger!" In combat, Johnson's legacy was established because he beat the "Great White Hope." Meanwhile, authorities worked hard to make his life more difficult.

Johnson was renowned for his lavish lifestyle, quickly indulging in luxuries and displaying opulence. He possessed flashy automobiles, enjoyed cigars, and had a taste for expensive wines and champagnes. It is worth noting that during an era marked by racial violence, segregation, and limited access to adequate facilities for African Americans, Johnson's preference for relationships predominantly leaned toward white women. Additionally, Johnson's life experiences contributed to his cultural refinement, evident in his avid reading of English, French, and Spanish novels. However, his arrogance and disregard for societal norms made him a highly sought-after individual during a time when racial injustices prevailed.

Consequently, the government made relentless efforts, employing legal and illegal means, to apprehend the boxing champion. In 1913, Jack Johnson was ultimately convicted on fabricated charges of violating the Mann Act, a law prohibiting the transportation of women across state lines for immoral purposes. He faced an eleven-count indictment, and a jury composed of white individuals swiftly found him guilty, resulting in a one-year prison sentence. However, Johnson defied the white establishment again by escaping to Mexico, Canada, and Europe while out on bail. It was only after seven years that he returned to fulfill his year-long sentence, despite the unjust nature of his conviction.

Johnson's historic bout against Jeffries catalyzed his enduring legacy, igniting a profound conflict between him and America's white society. Not only did Johnson become a prominent figure in the world of sports, but he also emerged as a significant political and social figure, likely becoming the most famous African American in the world during his prime. His accomplishments are commemorated for breaking the racial barriers in boxing, laying the groundwork for future great black heavyweight champions such as Joe Louis, Floyd Patterson, Sonny Liston, and Muhammad Ali. Although there were other black fighters, pervasive racist attitudes resurfaced when Jack Dempsey became the champion in 1919. After winning the heavyweight championship, Jack Dempsey's first public statement was, "I will pay no attention to Negro challengers." This statement epitomized the prevailing sentiment towards African Americans nationwide during the early 20th century. Considering this pervasive racism, it is truly remarkable to contemplate Johnson's achievements during that era. As the late sports journalist Dick Schaap expressed, when reflecting on Johnson, "Think of the forces that shaped him, of the time in which he lived, and accept one conclusion: He must have been some man."

Johnson's legacy served as a source of inspiration for future generations of African Americans, empowering them to challenge racism in the United States. By embodying a persona that defied white society through his prowess in boxing, Johnson laid the foundation for individuals like Muhammad Ali to confront segregation and Jim Crow laws, advancing the fight for equality. During Ali's peak, the famed actor James Earl Jones portrayed Johnson in the film The Great White Hope. Ali visited the film set and stated that his forced exile from boxing due to his unwillingness to fight in the Vietnam War was analogous to Johnson's exile from fighting in the United States owing to unlawful persecution by the federal government. "I grew to love the Jack Johnson image," Ali added, paying tribute to Johnson. I wanted to be harsh, strong, and arrogant, which white people didn't enjoy." Ali undoubtedly embraced this mindset and was willing to put Jim Crow traditions to the test in a way that America had never seen before. In doing so, he joined the Nation of Islam in 1964 and was rapidly connected with the group's leader, Elijah Muhammad, and prominent preacher Malcolm X.

CHAPTER THREE

MUHAMMAD ALI

It is crucial to recognize Muhammad Ali's stance on racial issues. Similar to Jack Johnson, Ali did not harbor hatred towards white individuals; rather, both men abhorred racism and the oppressive atmosphere of Jim Crow. Ali refused to accept a society that relegated African Americans to second-class citizenship. Throughout his life, Ali maintained friendships with individuals of all races. His resistance stemmed from his refusal to tolerate the mistreatment and discrimination that originated from the legacy of slavery. Like many young African Americans growing up in the 1950s, Ali's perception of racial matters was shattered when he witnessed the brutal murder of fourteen-year-old Emmett Till in 1955. Ali and Till were nearly the same age, and the sight of Till's disfigured face in an open casket profoundly impacted Ali. He felt a profound sense of disgust, sadness, and confusion, realizing the extent of hatred that some people were capable of.

It is important to note that Ali's decision to join the Nation of Islam was not driven by hate but rather by his deep commitment to faith and a quest for peace. However, he had a burning desire to confront and challenge racism in America. Ali's close friend and trainer, Angelo Dundee, who was white, spoke candidly about Ali's genuine character in 1964, stating, "If the Muslims teach hate, then Cassius is not a Muslim. This boy is incapable of hate. I think he is involved with these Muslims just because people don't want him to be." Muhammad Ali's ability to maintain a positive reception among many white individuals throughout his career, despite his affiliation with the controversial Nation of Islam, is particularly noteworthy. Understanding Ali's complex character requires careful interpretation and can be quite perplexing. During the 1960s, some argued that Ali harbored anti-American or anti-white sentiments, and one could make such arguments by selectively focusing on certain aspects of his rhetoric. In essence, Ali remained a constant work in progress throughout his more than fifty years in the public eye, which made him a challenging figure to fully comprehend. In his 1966 book titled "Black Is Best: The Riddle of Cassius Clay," author Jack Olsen sought to unravel the essence of Ali. In his exploration, Olsen discovered that Ali was an enigmatic individual, defying simple categorizations or definitive understanding:

> *Clay's personality is like a jigsaw puzzle whose pieces were cut by a drunken carpenter, a jumbled collection of moods and attitudes that do not seem to interlock. Sometimes, he sounds like a religious fanatic, his voice singsong and chanting, and all at once, he will turn into a calm, reasoning, if confused, student of the scriptures. He is a loudmouth windbag and, at the same time, a remarkably sincere and dedicated athlete. He can be a kindly benefactor of the neighborhood children and vicious bully in the ring, a prissy Puritan totally intolerant of drinkers and smokers, and a teller of dirty jokes.*

Olsen's struggle to reach a definitive assessment of Ali stems from Ali's belief that unconventional methods were necessary to achieve universally desirable outcomes. He faced criticism and disdain from some quarters because he defied traditional expectations in America. However, it can also be argued that Ali held controversial positions because he yearned for an America that upheld the fundamental values enshrined in its Declaration of Independence and Constitution.

During the 1960 Rome Olympics, Ali faced questions from a Soviet reporter about the racial climate in America. In response, he fiercely defended his country, stating, "Tell your readers we got qualified people working on that, and I'm not worried about the outcome. The U.S.A. is the best country in the world, counting yours. It may be hard to get something to eat sometimes, but I ain't fighting alligators and living in a mud hut." Ali was never hesitant to voice his opinions, whether in defense of America or in criticism of its questionable policies. The press in Rome even dubbed him "Uncle Sam's unofficial goodwill ambassador" and recognized his strong Americanism.

As an Olympic champion, Ali had an early platform to promote himself and express his convictions. The Olympic stage previewed the messages he would impart to the world in the following generation. Upon his return from Rome, Ali was greeted by his supporters at the Louisville airport, where he expressed himself through poetry:

> *To Make America the greatest is my goal So I beat the Russians, I beat the Pole, And the USA won the Medal of Gold Italians said, 'You're greater than the Cassius his old.' We like your name, we like your game, So make Rome your home, if you will. I said I appreciate your kind hospitality, But the USA is my country still 'cause they're waiting to welcome me in Louisville.*

Ali's amateur poetry at the Louisville airport gave a glimpse into his future talent for oral expression. While he didn't excel as a student in a formal educational setting, Ali embraced opportunities for intellectual growth through his daily interactions and relationships.

After his Olympic triumph, Ali's quest for knowledge expanded as he delved into studying Islam. He became increasingly frustrated by the sluggish pace of social progress in 1960s America. Despite his status as an Olympic champion and his unwavering patriotic fervor, Ali discovered that he was still regarded as a second-rate citizen in his hometown of Louisville. "I won a gold medal representing the United States at the Olympic Games, and when I came home to Louisville, I still got treated like a nigger. There were some restaurants I couldn't get served in. Some people kept calling me 'boy.'" In fact, many in Louisville simply referred to Ali as the "Olympic nigger."

Ali secretly started attending mosques with a clear mission to challenge racism in the United States. He would sneak into Nation of Islam meetings through the back door, not wanting people to know he was present. He feared that if his involvement became public, he would be barred from pursuing his goal of fighting for the championship title. Ali discovered a disciplined brotherhood within the mosques that opposed forced integration and advocated for black self-reliance through Islam. He encountered Muslims

Davis Truman 31

who questioned why black individuals were treated differently in America. These inquiries motivated him to break free from the lingering impact of slavery and strive for a different future.

Following the biggest fight of his young career in February 1964 against Sonny Liston for the heavyweight championship in Miami, Ali prepared to make a significant announcement regarding his religious conversion and name change. He created a spectacle leading up to the fight by boldly proclaiming that he would shock the world and pull off a major upset, aiming to draw attention to himself and boost ticket sales. His claims of shocking the world were not unfounded, as only three out of fifty-eight people polled at the fight believed that Ali would emerge victorious. Skeptics, including renowned columnist Jim Murray of the Los Angeles Times, doubted Ali's chances of success, comparing it to the understanding of Einstein's Theory. Comedian Jackie Gleason even predicted a quick victory for Liston, mocking Ali's bravado. Concerns for Ali's safety were legitimate among boxing enthusiasts. At the same time, rumors circulated about his affiliation with the Nation of Islam, particularly his association with

Malcolm X. The fight against Liston allowed Ali to reveal his conversion on the grandest stage possible.

Ali's global fame in the twentieth century can be attributed to his exceptional boxing skills and unparalleled verbal eloquence. The Liston fight showcased both aspects. He had a profound understanding of leveraging his physical talents to promote his image and advance his objectives through charismatic public displays. Ali utilized the platform provided to him to captivate audiences. At just twenty-two years old in February 1964, on the eve of his first championship fight against Liston, Ali displayed such confidence in himself that he boldly called out the skeptical media. He challenged them, saying, "It's your last chance to get on the bandwagon. I'm keeping a list of all you people." Ali was ready to impact the world and demonstrated his unwavering confidence by challenging the media to support him while he was still considered the underdog. Before the bout with Liston, Ali penned an article for Sports Illustrated titled "I'm a Little Special," showcasing his confrontational banter and showmanship. The title provides insight into Ali's confident and assertive attitude as a rising boxer from

Louisville. The article, as a whole, served as an introduction to the persona that the world would come to know well, a bold and dynamic young African American whom the magazine's editors described as a "loudmouth and braggart." Ali's unabashed self-praise and taunting of Liston left spectators astounded, as he had yet to prove himself in their eyes.

Liston, widely regarded as the most intimidating boxer of the time, was the clear favorite according to sportswriters. However, Ali sought every possible psychological advantage against him. Ali's impetuousness leading up to the fight reflected his awareness that a victory could mark the beginning of a historic career. At the same time, a loss could label him as a loudmouthed youngster overwhelmed by a superior opponent on a grand stage. His words before the Liston fight to exemplify this mindset, stating that if he were like many other heavyweight boxers, readers wouldn't be reading the article, highlighting his unique ability to engage with his charismatic style. Ali's cavalier attitude is evident throughout the article, reinforcing the magazine's cover that featured Ali gazing at the one million dollars he anticipated earning from the Liston fight. He confidently expressed, "I don't think it's bragging to say I'm something a little special." These words demonstrate his acute understanding of captivating the public's attention. He knew that regardless of whether they liked him, they would be captivated by his approach.

Ali was profoundly self-aware regarding his verbal prowess and its impact on his fame. He recognized that his ability to command attention through his words was instrumental in his success. Ali believed he might have been relegated to mediocrity without his charismatic and attention-grabbing persona. He acknowledged the potential outcome of a life washing windows or running an elevator, adhering to societal expectations, and suppressing his true self. Instead, he embraced his ability to captivate audiences, declaring himself one of the highest-paid athletes in the world and proclaiming himself the greatest fighter, all while acknowledging the significance of his accomplishments.

Ali's understanding of his own journey extended beyond personal fame. He recognized the historical plight of African Americans and sought to distance himself from the submissive responses of the past.

His refusal to conform to societal expectations of deference, symbolized by phrases like "yes suh" and "no such," was a deliberate choice to assert his individuality and break free from the remnants of slavery. His decision to change his name from Cassius Clay to Muhammad Ali reflected his desire to shed the name inherited from slave owners and establish his identity. Additionally, Ali revealed that his provocative criticism of Liston and the aggressive language he used were calculated strategies to generate interest in the fight. He openly admitted that his plan was to insult Liston to ignite conversations and build up the gate or ticket sales. This demonstrated Ali's keen understanding of public interest and ability to manipulate the media to market sporting events as major entertainment spectacles. His bold approach, particularly as an underdog attacking the formidable Liston, was unprecedented and generated significant attention and excitement for the fight.

Overall, Ali's self-awareness, ability to captivate audiences with his words, and strategic use of the media showcased his astute understanding of the social and cultural dynamics at play and his determination to transcend the limitations imposed on him. The buildup to the Clay-Liston fight served as a trial run for Ali's future approach to life. While he had already achieved some fame and notoriety through his Olympic victory and undefeated record, this fight marked his first significant professional challenge. Ali was determined to secure an opportunity to challenge the champion, and he approached the fight promotion with tremendous energy, testing the public's reaction to his bold tactics. His emotional intelligence and understanding of the public's response propelled him to a position where boxing promoters felt compelled to give him a shot at the title.

Ali recognized that simply relying on his boxing skills and staying quiet would not be enough to secure the opportunity he desired. He understood that he needed to generate buzz and capture public attention. He aimed to stand out and create a spectacle around himself by talking, screaming, and acting unconventionally. He knew his actions might lead some to view him as crazy or out of control. Still, he believed that the meaning behind his actions would ultimately bring him the desired notoriety and the chance to challenge Liston for the heavyweight title. Critics, such as New York Times columnist

Robert Lipsyte, initially questioned Ali's qualifications to step into the ring with Liston. They pointed out his lack of victories against significant opponents and his untested status. However, Ali's calculated antics and relentless self-promotion eventually fulfilled his goal, as he secured the opportunity to face Liston. These insights into Ali's mindset during this pivotal moment illuminated his strategic thinking and determination. He was willing to take risks, challenge conventional norms, and even face criticism to achieve his ambitions. This approach would become a defining characteristic of his life and career as he pushed boundaries inside and outside the boxing ring.

In the days leading up to the fight against Liston, Ali exuded a sense of confidence that often accompanies youth. While his confidence was not unfounded, his words had an element of naivety. Although Ali displayed some timidity and uncertainty, he was determined to prove his doubters wrong. He acknowledged that he heard voices telling him he couldn't do what he claimed, but he remained driven to "shock the world." His desire to prove himself motivated him to prepare tirelessly while also preparing for the possibility of losing the fight by contemplating alternative paths. Ali's fear of making it in something else outside of boxing did not become a reality. He achieved one of the greatest upsets in sports history by defeating Liston. The fight showcased Ali's superior speed, agility, and youth compared to the powerful Liston. During this historic moment, Ali uttered his famous words that resonated with the world: "I am the greatest! I shook up the world! I am the king of the world!" His victory transformed him into a global icon, bringing unparalleled boldness to his generation.

Ali understood that he was not a conventional athlete of the 1960s and embraced his uniqueness. He took pride in doing things differently, especially how he presented himself. This attitude and his willingness to challenge norms would become defining characteristics of his persona throughout his life and career. The morning after the fight, Cassius Clay proclaimed his new name Muhammad Ali. Reflecting on this year later, Ali expressed, "It freed me from the identity given to my family by my slave masters." This name change instilled fear in black and white individuals, signifying that the world champion would not conform to conventional norms. The name

Muhammad Ali carried a negative connotation due to the strong language associated with Black Muslims. Despite this, Ali vehemently rejected joining a separatist hate group and asserted, "I like everybody; I treat everybody right," when challenged by a reporter.

Ali observed that he quickly transitioned from being an intriguing braggart to an "evil man" in white circles, stating, "I got bad all of a sudden." Upon his return to New York's Madison Square Garden, Ali sought a hero's welcome but was met with overwhelming boos because he insisted on being introduced by his new name. The white media and black civil rights advocates refused to refer to him as Muhammad Ali. Prominent boxing sportswriter Jimmy Cannon criticized Ali for his affiliation with Black Muslims, accusing him of weaponizing boxing as an instrument of hate and attacking the spirit.

Nevertheless, Ali remained resolute in his decision to shed the slave name Cassius Clay and embrace Muhammad Ali as he pursued a future marked by social activism. Despite newspaper editors discouraging using his new name, Ali was infuriated when interviewers addressed him as Cassius Clay. On one occasion, he admonished a reporter, declaring, "I'm not Cassius... you wanna keep calling me a white man's name. I'm not white. I don't wanna be called by your name no more. I'm no slave. I'm Muhammad Ali."

Furthermore, he proudly asserted, "I believe in Allah and in peace... I'm not a Christian anymore," reflecting a shift in his religious beliefs since his baptism at twelve. At the age of twenty-two, Ali had astounded the world and found himself able to influence millions. His intentions were clear as he boldly proclaimed, "I am America. I am the part you won't recognize but get used to me. Black, confident, cocky. My name, not yours. My religion, not yours. My goals, my own. Get used to me."

CHAPTER FOUR

FROM CASSIUS CLAY TO MUHAMMAD ALI

Ali's conversion to Islam sparked significant controversy in the mainstream media, yet it also shaped him into an iconic figure. As the world's heavyweight champion, his religious affiliation became a prominent aspect of his public persona. Discussing a boxer's religion had never been such a profound subject before. Still, Ali's association with the Nation of Islam and its confrontational rhetoric subjected him to unparalleled scrutiny. Despite the backlash, Ali passionately expressed his newfound faith:

> *I ain't no Christian. I can't be when I see all the colored people fighting for forced integration getting [blown] up. They get hit by stones and chewed by dogs, and they blow up a Negro church and don't find the killers. I get*

telephone calls every day. They want me to carry signs. They want me to picket. They tell me it would be a wonderful thing if I married a white woman because this would be good for brotherhood. I don't want to be washed down sewers. I just want to be happy with my own kind.

In 1960, Ali developed a deep fascination with Islam when he was introduced to a mosque by a minister. Within the mosque walls, he encountered teachings that shed light on the historical struggles faced by African Americans, particularly their identity being stripped away during the brutal era of slavery and their forced assimilation into white culture. The mosque became where Ali discovered his own truth, leading him to embrace the religion and reject the slave name imposed on his family for generations. It was either an extraordinary stroke of luck or an exceptional foresight that Ali foresaw his conversion as a path to transcendent status. In 1964, he confidently declared, "my change is one of the things that will mark me as a great man in history."

Throughout his conversion, Ali skillfully intertwined peace and Islam, even amid the militant atmosphere surrounding Black Muslims. This might seem contradictory to some, but it directly reflected his core beliefs. He vehemently objected to any insinuation of hate being associated with his faith early on, stating, "People brand us a hate group... That is not true. Followers of Allah are the sweetest people in the world... They pray five times a day... All they want to do is live in peace." As Ali matured and developed, his devotion to his faith grew stronger. In the months leading up to the fight against Liston, he formed a special bond with Malcolm X. Malcolm X, serving as the primary representative of the Nation of Islam in the early 1960s, had been assigned to Ali by the self-proclaimed prophet Elijah Muhammad. In his Autobiography, Malcolm X expressed a deep hatred towards Liston and Patterson, who had "white priests" as their spiritual advisors in their camps.

Malcolm X made it clear to Ali that the fight against Liston carried significant religious implications and symbolized the struggle of Muslims worldwide. He said, "This fight is the truth. The Cross and the Crescent are fighting in a prize ring for the first time. It's a modern Crusade, a Christian, and a Muslim facing each other with television to beam it off Telstar for the whole world to see what happens! Do you think Allah has brought about all this intending for you to leave the ring as anything but the champion?"Ali took this message to heart and was determined to represent his adopted organization and its faith with the utmost integrity.

Furthermore, Malcolm X echoed Ali's declarations during press conferences that it had been "prophesied" for him to emerge victorious. Elijah Muhammad, filled with pride and delight, openly expressed his satisfaction with the newest member of his group rising to the top of the boxing world after Ali triumphed over Liston. He remarked, "The enemy wanted him to come out all blasted. They had said that Liston would tear up that pretty face of yours. But Allah and I said, 'no, no.'" It was clear that Elijah Muhammad, Malcolm X, and Ali shared a profound spiritual connection to the victory over Liston.

Elijah Muhammad's influence on Ali had a profound impact. The teachings of the Nation of Islam made Ali question many of his earlier thoughts on race and religion while growing up in Louisville. Shortly after his conversion, Ali reflected, "When I went to church on Sunday, I always asked my mother, 'how come is everything white?' I said, 'why is Jesus white with blond hair and blue eyes? Angels were white.' I knew something was wrong, but I couldn't pinpoint it." As Ali contemplated these thought-provoking questions, the media and many white Americans intensified their mockery of the new champion. They had hoped that Ali would conform to the expected role of an African-American hero, as Joe Louis had done in the 1930s and 1940s. However, Ali defied almost every expectation. Salim Muwakkil, former editor of the Nation of Islam newspaper Muhammad Speaks, recalled, "It was an affront to many Americans that the heavyweight champion of the world would reject American identity and all that entailed for something as obscure and cultish as the Nation of Islam."

Undeterred by the criticism, Ali remained resolute in his partnership with the Nation of Islam to challenge the deep-seated racism in America. He understood that boxing, compared to the global phenomenon of religion, was a mere pursuit, and this realization contributed to his worldwide impact. 1964 he acknowledged, "My being a Muslim moved me from the sports pages to the front pages. I'm a much bigger man than I would be if I were a champion prizefighter. Twenty-four hours a day, I get offers to tour somewhere overseas, visit colleges, and make speeches. Places like Harvard and Tuskegee, television shows, interviews, and recordings. I get letters from all over." Ali relished the attention because it allowed him to impact the world beyond the realm of a traditional boxing champion like Patterson or Liston. At the young age of twenty-two in 1964, Ali's growing social significance was unimaginable. John McDermott, a writer for Life Magazine, recognized that Ali's greatness was only beginning to be unveiled but sensed that "at a minimum, he is going to be one of the most controversial figures in the whole array of heavyweight champions." It was evident that Ali was destined to be more than just another champion. While his stage was boxing, the world knew him as a champion in the ring and a leading advocate for racial and social justice, revered worldwide. However, this reverence did not come without intense criticism for his association with

Elijah Muhammad's separatist Nation of Islam. The traditionalists in the media relentlessly disparaged the new champion, prompting a cynical response from Malcolm X: "If he was white, they would be referring to him as the 'All-American boy.'"

Over time, Ali utilized his religious principles and social standing to be inclusive, forging relationships and partnerships with people of all backgrounds and becoming a leader in humanitarian causes. Ali was destined for greatness, as affirmed by his beloved trainer, Angelo Dundee, who eloquently stated in 1964, "working with Cassius and going along with him is like watching a beautiful movie, and you are a witness to its making... I never met anyone like him, and I know I never will again." Dundee remained close to Ali throughout his career, and his sentiments reflected a world that would become enamored with Ali for the next half-century as he emerged as one of the most admired figures on the planet. While Ali embodied an intense and uncommon rhetorical style among African Americans in the 1960s, his rival Floyd Patterson aligned himself with Martin Luther King Jr.'s nonviolent approach. Patterson shared King's belief that "a doctrine of black supremacy is as dangerous as a doctrine of white supremacy." He symbolized the movement toward integration and used his platform in boxing to promote harmonious relations between black and white communities.

On the contrary, Ali was unwilling to take the gradual path toward racial equality. He was eager to expose the injustices of Jim Crow racism and criticize those within the black community whom he believed were compliant with white society, labeling them as "Uncle Toms." Ali aimed to awaken America's black community to active resistance, stating, "Most black people in this country are mentally dead, and we don't wake up easy. It takes something like an earthquake to wake up our people. Maybe black folks will get upset about something and burn a building or two, but we forget in a couple of days." His repeated call was for black people to actively challenge racism instead of employing passive resistance, asking, "Why are we called Negroes? Why are we deaf, dumb, and blind? Why is everybody making progress, yet we lag so far behind?" Ali frequently referred to Patterson as an "Uncle Tom" and did not show him respect, leading to a heated rivalry between the fighters.

Less than a year after Ali's victory over Liston in February 1964, Patterson wrote an article with writer Milton Gross for Sports Illustrated, expressing his desire to have a chance to fight the champion. In his piece titled "I Want to Destroy Clay," Patterson launched various attacks on Ali, including critiques of his character. Patterson saw himself as an example of a more sophisticated African American than Ali and Liston. He subtly portrayed Liston as a brutish, uneducated black man and depicted Ali as a bold, militant young fighter unworthy of being a champion. For instance, Patterson highlighted Liston's criminal history and Ali's association with Black Muslims. Patterson adamantly refused to refer to the champion as Muhammad Ali, insisting on calling him Cassius Clay while proudly proclaiming himself a "life member" of the NAACP. His sentiments were clear as he claimed to be superior to both Liston and Ali in his contribution to the African American community: "[The NAACP] felt that if [Liston] became the champion, he could bring discredit to the Negroes' position... and [Ali has] practically turned the title over to the Black Muslims. Because of that, I can't respect him as a champion or a man."

Patterson firmly believed it was his duty to reclaim the title from the Black Muslims and restore it to a place where an integrated community could take pride in its champion. This confrontational language only reinforced Ali's assertion that Patterson was a pawn of the white community. Patterson's disdain for Black Muslims was so strong that he condemned the entire organization, equating them to the Ku Klux Klan. In 1963, Patterson openly expressed, "I have no respect for the Black Muslims. They're a colored Ku Klux Klan." He argued that Ali had been manipulated by the group, which embarrassed the black community. Patterson's motivation to fight Ali and regain the championship was so intense that he even suggested, "Maybe the Black Muslims would repudiate him [and] it could be my small contribution to civil rights." The animosity between Patterson and Ali extended far beyond the boxing ring; their rhetoric reflected their personal differences and their respective views on black America. In their subsequent fights, Ali humiliated Patterson by prolonging the matches to inflict more punishment while chastising him as an "Uncle Tom." In a broader context, they represented divergent voices within the civil rights movement, with Patterson aligning more closely with the popular nonviolent approach. At the same time, Ali embraced the more militant rhetoric of Black Nationalism.

George Plimpton, a prominent writer, closely followed Ali's career and developed a strong relationship with him early on during his conversion to Islam. Plimpton spent time with Ali shortly after his victory over Liston in 1964 and was captivated by the boxer from the beginning. He marveled at how even the simplest questions from reporters would lead to a spectacle: "[Ali would] unleash an act, an entertainment which included poetry... not a dull show by any standard, even if you've seen it a few times before." Ali's ability to consistently entertain and impress while discussing weighty subjects like race and religion amplified his impact on people wherever he went. His innate gift for captivating audiences allowed his words to resonate with diverse individuals worldwide.

During Plimpton's time in Miami covering the Liston fight, he had the chance to meet Malcolm X for the first time. Malcolm X was part of Ali's entourage, and rumors were circulating about Cassius Clay's conversion to the Nation of Islam and his name change to Muhammad Ali. Ali and Malcolm X were inseparable before the Liston fight, and their bond was so strong that Ferdie Pacheco, Ali's physician, likened them to "very close brothers" or even two people in love. Plimpton was immediately impressed by Malcolm X, viewing him as a "true revolutionary" who expressed his opinions without hesitation. Plimpton couldn't help but draw a rhetorical parallel between the young fighter and the intellectual revolutionary, noting that neither stumbled over words or ideas, giving the sense that their minds were engaged in rote playback rather than active thinking. The comparison to Malcolm X is intriguing because it highlights Ali's unwavering confidence in his oratory skills. Despite his boisterous demeanor, Ali possessed intellectual depth that challenged even the most academic minds to articulate his ideas. Malcolm X, for his part, was not primarily interested in Ali as an athlete but as a thinker, recognizing the untapped mental energy and intellectual prowess he possessed. He even remarked that Ali should be a diplomat. This statement proved remarkably prescient given Ali's later humanitarian endeavors and meetings with heads of state over the next fifty years.

When George Plimpton asked Malcolm X if he was teaching Ali to have a militant Islamic mindset, Malcolm X quickly responded by saying, "He will make up his own mind," emphasizing that Ali was an independent thinker who could evolve based on his core values and the contemporary issues he faced. Even before Malcolm X softened his stance on race issues, he highlighted in a 1963 interview the Nation of Islam's fundamental core values of freedom, justice, and equality as being more moderate: "Freedom, justice, and equality are our principal ambitions." Ali, in turn, never fully embraced discourse that portrayed whites as devils. However, Malcolm X and the leaders of the Nation of Islam recognized Ali's value to their movement and utilized him to advance their cause. For example, just two days after the Liston fight, Malcolm X interrupted Ali during a press conference to defend his conversion, stating that Ali would mean more to his people than any athlete before him. He emphasized that Ali was the black man's hero, contrasting him with Jackie Robinson, who was seen as the white man's hero. Malcolm X claimed that the white press wanted Ali to lose because of his Muslim faith, while they didn't care about the religion of other athletes. Although Ali conformed to the Nation of Islam's party line, his true nature was universal acceptance towards everyone. Ali longed for peace and didn't believe in forcing himself on white people. He clarified that he didn't hate white people and understood their history. Unfortunately, Ali was influenced by the racial tensions of the 1950s and 1960s and believed that change would come through direct confrontation. As a result, he openly confronted racism with aggressive language early in his public life. However, his open-mindedness became more apparent in his positions once the turbulence of the 1960s began to subside.

After the Liston fight, Ali and Malcolm X spent several days together. Malcolm X shared his knowledge of the Quran with Ali and continued educating him on race and the Nation of Islam. They embarked on a journey from Miami to New York and encountered the difficulties of finding a meal in the racially segregated Deep South. Reflecting on the experience, Ali expressed his disappointment in poetic form, stating, "Man, it was really a letdown drag/For all those miles I had to eat out of a bag." Upon arriving in New York, they walked into Times Square after dinner, where Ali was amazed by Malcolm X's popularity. He told reporters, "Malcolm X got more requests for his autograph than I did. He's the greatest."

Similarly, Malcolm X deeply admired the champion, believing Ali was uniquely positioned to restore racial pride among African Americans and worldwide. Their bond grew stronger as they visited the United Nations, where Ali attracted significant attention with his bold claim of being the king of the world. Foreign diplomats and American representatives responded with a mixture of annoyance and fascination.

However, their time together came to an unfortunate end due to Malcolm X's falling out with Nation of Islam leader Elijah Muhammad. Soon after, Malcolm X was dismissed from the Nation of Islam, causing a rift between him and Ali. Elijah Muhammad ordered his officials to harm or kill anyone who left the sect to follow Malcolm X heightened tensions. Malcolm X himself warned of this just weeks before his assassination. The unsolved assassination, widely believed to be carried out by the Nation of Islam, occurred on February 21, 1965. While Ali publicly supported the Nation of Islam, privately, he feared for his safety due to his association with Malcolm X and the Muslims. He couldn't openly express the remorse he felt for his estranged friend. Even Ali's mother, Odessa Clay, spoke out after the assassination, expressing concern for her son's well-being and her disapproval of the organization he had joined. At only twenty-three years old during Malcolm X's death, Ali remained unwavering in his commitment to the Nation of Islam under the influence of Elijah Muhammad. However, he did not endorse violence. Ali continued emphasizing the need for black independence and self-reliance to challenge the racist system.

"The Nation of Islam was a controversial organization known for its militant rhetoric and Elijah Muhammad's call for racial separation. This naturally created tensions within both the black and white communities. White Americans were offended by being labeled as the 'devil' by Black Muslims. At the same time, even some members of the mainstream black community found the Nation of Islam's positions at odds with the civil rights movement's goals. However, Muhammad Ali was a complex and evolving figure. Despite his affiliation with the Nation of Islam, he maintained relationships with diverse people and had a knack for connecting with individuals from all backgrounds. This included blacks and whites from around the world. Though not universally embraced, his decision to join the Nation of Islam evoked a sense of admiration and excitement among some African Americans.

Julian Bond, a prominent civil rights leader, and future politician, expressed a positive view of Ali's decision to join the Nation of Islam. He acknowledged that while many may not have liked the act of joining, the fact that Ali boldly aligned himself with a despised group in mainstream America sent a thrilling message. It represented a willingness to challenge societal norms and stand proudly in his convictions. Other African Americans, such as Jill Nelson, a well-known black journalist, shared similar sentiments. Their reactions reflected a mixture of appreciation for Ali's fearlessness and an understanding that his actions carried symbolic weight. Despite the controversy surrounding the Nation of Islam, Ali's commitment to his beliefs resonated with many within the black community, even if they didn't fully align with the organization's ideology." Notably, perspectives on Ali's association with the Nation of Islam varied among individuals and communities, and opinions could differ widely. The well-known black journalist Jill Nelson expressed,

> *We weren't about to join the Nation, but we loved Ali for that supreme act of defiance. It was the defiance against having to be the good Negro, the good Christian waiting to be rewarded by the righteous white provider. We loved Ali because he was so beautiful and powerful and because he talked a lot of lip. But he also epitomized a lot of black people's emotions at the time, our anger, our sense of entitlement, the need to be better just to get to the median, and the sense of standing up against the furies.*

Indeed, Muhammad Ali's words and actions brought a sense of hope and renewed confidence to many people in the black community during a time when progress in civil rights was being met with slow implementation and enforcement. Ali's approach was distinct and daring, standing out from the conventional methods of the civil rights movement. Ali's outspokenness and unapologetic self-expression resonated with those frustrated by the gradual pace of change. He was not afraid to challenge societal norms, whether through his provocative statements on racial issues, his refusal to be drafted into the Vietnam War, or his affiliation with the Nation of Islam. Ali's boldness in expressing his beliefs and willingness to face the consequences endeared him to many in the black community seeking a fresh approach to advancing their rights and dignity.

Ali's words and actions were seen as new and bold because he represented a departure from the civil rights movement leaders' more restrained and measured strategies. He embraced his role as a public figure and used his platform to champion the cause of racial equality and justice. His charisma, poetic eloquence, and unyielding spirit inspired many who yearned for a more assertive and uncompromising stance in pursuing civil rights. Ali became an emblematic black empowerment and pride figure by embodying courage and resilience. He demonstrated that one could be unapologetically black, confident, and successful, challenging the prevailing narratives and stereotypes. Ali's impact went beyond the boxing ring, as his words and actions resonated with people in the black community who were seeking a voice of their own, someone who would fearlessly confront the obstacles and demand equal treatment and respect. In this way, Muhammad Ali provided a source of hope and a renewed sense of confidence to individuals in the black community who felt stagnant in the face of slow progress. His audacity, charisma, and unwavering commitment to his beliefs inspired many to embrace their agency and continue the struggle for equality with renewed vigor.

CHAPTER FIVE

THE CHAMPION OF SOCIAL JUSTICE

Muhammad Ali's alignment with the Nation of Islam and his outspokenness on issues of race and social justice served as a catalyst for change. It inspired other African-American athletes and prominent figures to reconsider their role in advocating for equality. Jackie Robinson, who broke the color barrier in Major League Baseball, recognized the impact of Ali's message and appreciated the importance of black individuals recognizing their greatness and worth. A sociologist and activist, Harry Edwards worked with African-American athletes during the 1960s, including Tommie Smith and John Carlos, who famously raised their fists in a Black Power salute at the 1968 Olympics. Edwards credited Ali for giving these athletes the confidence to make such a political statement. Stokely Carmichael, a prominent civil rights activist, acknowledged Ali's influence on their movement and stated that athletes like Smith and Carlos were joining Ali as heroes who prioritized the concerns of black people over sports.

However, there were also athletes like O.J. Simpson, who, despite being a successful black athlete, distanced himself from issues of race and activism. Simpson's statement, "I'm not black; I'm O.J.," reflects the sentiment that Ali challenged, namely the need for black individuals to embrace their identity and use their platform to address social injustices. In this way, Ali's unapologetic stance and ability to challenge the prevailing norms and expectations inspired others to reconsider their roles and responsibilities in advocating for change and equality. His influence extended beyond the boxing ring, making him a powerful civil rights activist and a catalyst for social transformation. Jim Brown, the renowned athlete, and actor, shared a similar perspective to Muhammad Ali regarding the Nation of Islam. While Brown did not convert to the faith like Ali, he acknowledged the organization's role in instilling pride and self-reliance among black people. Brown believed that the Nation of Islam exposed the racism prevalent in white America and taught black individuals to uplift themselves. He argued that the media's negative portrayal of Black Muslims resulted from white America's discomfort in confronting its racist tendencies.

Although the Nation of Islam faced significant criticism during the 1960s, historical revisionists recognize Ali's role in advancing the cause of civil rights through his association with the organization. Even during his loyalty to Elijah Muhammad and the Nation of Islam, Ali implicitly advocated for the civil rights movement. Despite his initial criticism of the movement, Ali gained the respect of civil rights leaders like Martin Luther King, Jr. and became a guide for furthering their cause. He took a different path but acknowledged his respect for leaders like King. Bryant Gumbel, a prominent journalist who eulogized Ali in 2016, reflected on Ali's impact on the civil rights movement. Gumbel, an African American who valued the civil rights movement, believed that Ali's refusal to be afraid inspired black Americans to overcome their fears. Watching Ali's fearlessness, people gained the courage to continue fighting for justice and equality. Ali's influence extended beyond those directly associated with the Nation of Islam, resonating with individuals of different backgrounds who shared his disdain for injustice and inequality.

In this way, Ali's defiance and refusal to back down in the face of injustice inspired others, regardless of their affiliation with the Nation of Islam, to stand up for their rights and fight for a more just society. His impact reached beyond racial and religious boundaries, uniting people against oppression and fueling the ongoing struggle for equality. Uring the turbulent 1960s, Muhammad Ali's decision to make Harlem his home after his first fight against Sonny Liston was considered a deliberate choice to be among his black brethren. Ali wanted to live in a neighborhood where he could be close to fellow African Americans and experience the community's struggles and triumphs firsthand. In contrast, he openly mocked Floyd Patterson, another prominent black boxer, for moving his family to a predominantly white suburb in an attempt to integrate into upper-middle-class society. Ali's decision to reside in Harlem resonated with his contemporaries, and he became a source of immense pride during those challenging times. Gil Noble, a popular black journalist, recalled Ali's significance and the pride he instilled within the African American community. Ali's unapologetic stance and refusal to conform to societal expectations symbolized the spirit of resistance and empowerment prevalent during the era.

By choosing to live in Harlem, Ali not only expressed his solidarity with his black brethren but also immersed himself in the realities and experiences of the community. His presence in Harlem and his unyielding determination to fight for justice and equality uplifted and inspired many, serving as a powerful symbol of black pride and resilience during intense racial tension and social change. Muhammad Ali's influence extended beyond the boundaries of inner cities and reached even the elite corners of American society. One example is Jeremy Hubball, a white student at Groton School, an exclusive prep school in Massachusetts. Groton School, known for its association with America's elite, emphasized gentility, sportsmanship, and a system derived from British aristocracy. Hubball, who was about to graduate from Groton in 1965, became captivated by Ali shortly before he departed. Witnessing Ali's first victory over Liston in 1964, Hubball was struck by the boxer's audacity and defiance. Ali, a smart and irreverent black man, demanded attention and challenged the norms of the civil rights leaders who distanced themselves from his flamboyant and polarizing posture. Ali's intrusion on a prestigious institution like Groton represented his larger impact on America, affecting black and white communities. His rhetoric was compelling and more emphatic as his success in the ring increased.

Ali's rise to prominence perplexed students like Hubball, who were immersed in a privileged educational environment where white superiority was the norm. They faced the challenge of reconciling their traditional worldview with Ali's unapologetic style. Hubball acknowledged the smugness, condescension, and noblesse oblige that permeated their privileged world view. In contrast, Martin Luther King, Jr.'s visit to Groton in February 1963 had been more readily accepted by many students, as King represented the African American struggle in a manner that aligned with their ideals of social justice. Ali's approach, on the other hand, with his distinctive style and rhetoric, was perceived as more threatening and less palatable to some members of the Groton community. Ali's impact on American society was complex and multifaceted, challenging preconceived notions and pushing boundaries in black and white communities. His unapologetic self-expression and defiance of societal expectations forced individuals, even those in privileged and traditionally conservative environments, to confront their beliefs and biases.

In May 1965, just before Jeremy Hubball graduated from Groton School, he was invited to listen to the second Ali-Liston fight on the radio in the study of the school's headmaster, Reverend Jack Crocker. Reverend Crocker, an advocate for civil rights, had a prominent presence at the Episcopal school and spoke of "muscular Christianity" to his students. Hubball gathered with his peers by the radio, feeling nervous and excited. The fight ended quickly with Ali's victory in the first round, leaving Hubball elated but hesitant to express his enthusiasm in front of his respected headmaster. To Hubball, Ali represented something electrifying and promising, a hint of a new kind of danger. Ali's charisma was undeniable, but his behavior and brashness clashed with the refined sensibilities fostered at Groton.

Mischief, bravado, and disobedience were not tolerated in the school's environment. Despite the contradictions, Ali's appeal to Hubbell and his generation signified change and a future of social justice. Inspired by Ali's momentum, black and white individuals brought their energy to college campuses and cities across America, channeling the spirit of transformation. During the turbulent 1960s, the older generation, shaped by World War II, questioned the significance of Ali's bravado. Was he merely a buffoon or a symbol of originality? What kind of change did he represent? Regardless, Ali's unique combination of humor and boldness captivated the new generation. Black individuals were proud to have someone standing up for them with such passion, while white individuals rocked with excitement, seeing in Ali the embodiment of the change they desired. For young white men like Randy Roberts, an Ali historian, Ali became the unofficial spokesman of their generation, an inconceivable notion that reflected the power of Ali to inspire others with his passion and powerful rhetoric. Ali represented hope and confidence for the change people longed to see, making him the era's epitome.

Between his fights with Liston in February 1964 and March 1965, Muhammad Ali experienced a significant boost in his notoriety. As the world heavyweight champion, Ali used his newfound platform to voice his opinions on social issues and promote his faith, Islam. He recognized that his conversion to Islam resonated with Muslims worldwide, and he embraced his new identity as Muhammad Ali, shedding his birth name of Cassius Clay. Ali understood that his global fame would allow him to travel and connect with people from various countries to discuss freedom, justice, and equality. Although Ali had already gained some fame by winning a gold medal in the 1960 Rome Olympics, his reputation skyrocketed in 1964. He capitalized on his newfound recognition and embarked on a five-week international tour, visiting Africa and the Middle East. Ali was received with overwhelming enthusiasm in countries like Ghana, Nigeria, and Egypt. Banners and signs proclaimed his greatness and welcomed him as a hero. Maya Angelou, living in Ghana then, recalled Ali's ecstatic reception and the chants of "Ali, the Greatest!" that filled the streets. Ali proudly embraced his African heritage and proclaimed himself an African with his new name, Muhammad Ali. For decades, the tour served as a foundation for his worldwide renown, captivating citizens globally. Ali reveled in the adoration he received, considering himself the first world champion to embark on a global tour as a champion of the people. His journey across Africa and the Middle East further solidified his commitment to Islam and validated his decision to embrace the religion.

Muhammad Ali was genuinely amazed by the excitement he elicited in Africa and Asia. He was surprised to be embraced as their champion in Ghana, Nigeria, Pakistan, and Turkey. The magnitude of his celebrity and the fact that people from all walks of life knew him deeply moved him. Ali acknowledged the weight of his fame and the need to set an example of good living for the world that watched him. He was particularly struck by the outpouring of support from the villages and hills of Africa, where everyone recognized and revered him. His friend, Malcolm X, recognized the symbolic importance of Ali's trip and advised him to be aware of his tremendous responsibilities to the billions of people in Africa, Arabia, and Asia who loved him blindly. Ali took this advice to heart and understood the need to protect the positive image he had among his people. The journey to Africa and Asia deepened Ali's cultural awareness and pride in his African heritage. He embraced the history and culture of Africa and returned to America with a renewed sense of African pride, aiming to combat the shame of slavery. He proudly proclaimed that his name, Muhammad Ali, resonated worldwide, particularly in Ethiopia, Morocco, Syria, Indonesia, Pakistan, Turkey, Algiers, and Saudi Arabia. The trip allowed him to build new relationships and leave millions of devoted fans behind at every stop. Upon his return to New York, Ali spoke of being mobbed and the overwhelming response he received from people, with women and children even jumping off roofs to catch a glimpse of him. This trip profoundly impacted Ali's global reach and solidified his legacy as an international icon.

Muhammad Ali naturally attracted attention and captivated crowds wherever he went. He acknowledged that he had been drawing attention since he could walk and talk. Poetry became a tool for him to express himself and provoke his opponents. Even during his amateur days in Louisville, he would use poetic taunts before fights, such as predicting a quick victory. As he transitioned into a professional boxer, Ali recognized that his talking and poetry psychologically impacted his opponents, unsettling them before the fights. It became an integral part of his persona and a way to assert his confidence. While there is no definitive research on Ali being the most quoted poet in history, he is widely known for his poetic expressions. In an interview with Alex Haley of Playboy in October 1964, Ali boldly claimed that his poetry gets printed and quoted more than professional poets favored by critics. He disregarded critics' opinions, asserting that if they truly understood their craft, they should be doing it instead of criticizing from the sidelines. Ali's audacity in making such a claim at the age of twenty-two in 1964 is remarkable. However, he had unique foresight, recognizing that his words would resonate beyond his era. His poetry and eloquence contributed to his enduring legacy and ability to profoundly connect with people.

Ali's career began with bombastic rhetoric and vernacular poetry. Poetry aided him in becoming an engaging speaker, establishing him as an authoritative voice on significant social concerns. Ali, for example, used amusing poetry to provoke Liston before their fight in 1964:

> *Clay comes out to meet Liston, and Liston starts to retreat. If Liston goes back an inch farther, he'll end up in a ringside seat. Clay swings with his left, and Clay swings with his right, Look at young Cassius carrying the fight; Liston keeps backing, but there's not enough room. It's a matter of time till Clay lowers the boom. Now Clay lands with a right, what a beautiful swing, And the punch raises the Bear to clean out the ring. Liston is still rising, and the ref frowns, For he can't start counting till Sonny goes down. Now Liston is disappearing from view, and the crowd is going frantic, But radar stations have picked him up somewhere over the Atlantic. Who would have thought when they came to the fight? That they'd witness the launching of a human satellite. Yes, the crowd did not dream, when they put up the money, That they would see a total eclipse of Sonny.*

Muhammad Ali's prowess as a wordsmith extended beyond mere amateurism, despite his unconventional style and playful taunts. His words were widely reported and quoted, and his claim of being the most cited poet of his era holds some truth. Renowned poet LeRoi Jones, writing in 1964, acknowledged that Ali's blustering and playground poetry were valid expressions that resonated with a new and more complex generation. Ali's verbal brilliance went beyond taunting his opponents; it reflected his charismatic and eloquent nature. In 1968, sports journalist Bud Collins even compared Ali to the great poet Robert Frost, suggesting that Ali may have been the greatest poet since Frost himself. Notably, Ali's words were entertaining and powerful messages, often infused with insightful humor. He used his platform to elevate black pride and inspire African Americans, becoming a leader in the fight for social justice. Even during his exile from boxing, Ali was invited to speak at numerous college commencements, where he delivered speeches that motivated and empowered graduates. Muhammad Ali's ability to combine humor, insight, and social commentary in his speeches and poetry made him an influential figure, resonating with people across generations and establishing his legacy as a legendary athlete, powerful communicator, and advocate for change. On one such occasion, Ali accentuated the beauty of blackness:

> *I'm not just saying black is best because I'm black. I can prove it. If you want some rich dirt, you look for the black dirt. If you want the best bread, you want the whole wheat rye bread. Costs more money, but it's better for your digestive system. You want the best sugar for cooking; it's brown sugar. The blacker the berry, the sweeter the fruit. If I want a strong cup of coffee, I'll take it black. The coffee gets weak if I integrate it with white cream.*

These statements to college graduates exemplify Ali's superb oratory mechanism: the blend of fun and message. It is a powerful demonstration of why so many young blacks were smitten with him and felt pride in his example. Furthermore, he could effortlessly invert the message above to stress that a "brainwashing" had occurred for hundreds of years to make people believe that white was better than black, as he does in the following address:

Everything good is supposed to be white. We look at Jesus, and we see a white with blond hair and blue eyes. I'm sure there's a heaven in the sky, and colored folks die and go to heaven. Where are the colored angels? They must be in the kitchen preparing milk and honey. We look at Miss America. We see white. We look at Miss World. We see white. We look at Miss Universe, and we see white. Even Tarzan, the king of the jungle in black Africa, he's white. White Owl Cigars. White Swan soap. White Cloud tissue paper, White Rain hair rinse, White Tornado floor wax. All the good cowboys ride the white horses and wear white hats. Angel food cake is a white cake, but the [devil's] food cake is chocolate. When are we going to wake up as a people and end the lie that white is better than black?

The richness of Ali's discourse then and throughout his life was a source of pride for millions. Ali's ideas encouraged blacks all over America; he was original and not afraid to be a pioneer for black growth. Ferdie Pacheco, Ali's white doctor, was particularly moved by Ali's ability to inspire and transform America's perspective of black people:

Blacks were considered subhuman—hard word for me to say, but that's what they were. In the South especially. That's where Ali's from, in the South. He comes along, and by dint of his athletic ability, his graciousness, his funniness, his personality, and this incredibly good-looking body and face, he says to the camera, 'Black is beautiful. Look at me. I'm prettier than anybody in Hollywood . . . and I'm black.' . . . By the time he got through, he had defused the idea that black was ugly. 'You don't have to worry about being black. Black is beautiful.' And in that context alone, if you didn't look at anything else, he was just as big as Martin Luther King or anybody else 'cause he got black people thinking that they were good, nay, that they were better.

Muhammad Ali's impact on changing the perception of being black was remarkable and far-reaching. It was not limited to a specific region or group within America but resonated with a diverse range of people worldwide. In doing so, Ali carved out his own unique place within the intellectual continuum of black thinkers, alongside the more traditional rhetoric of figures like Martin Luther King

Jr. Ali used his platform as a renowned athlete to champion social causes and promote religious freedom. When faced with the threat of losing his title due to his affiliation with the Nation of Islam, Ali staunchly defended his right to practice his chosen religion, emphasizing the principles of religious freedom in America. He firmly believed that everyone should be free to practice their religion or even have no religion if desired.

For Ali, his religious convictions held greater significance than his boxing career. He expressed willingness to quit fighting altogether if it meant compromising his religious beliefs. He recognized that his role outside the ring, advocating for the rights and equality of his black brothers and sisters struggling for their human rights in America, was of far greater importance. Ali saw himself as fighting a larger battle for social justice and was prepared to sacrifice for the cause. By the mid-1960s, Ali had laid the foundation for a lifetime of public advocacy and uniting people across the globe. His unwavering commitment to his beliefs, dedication to promoting social justice, and ability to inspire others made him an iconic figure who transcended the realm of sports and became a symbol of resistance, courage, and determination.

Ali's evolving views on integration and his desire for peace are evident even during his affiliation with the Nation of Islam and his association with Elijah Muhammad. In a 1967 interview, Ali expressed his liberal stance on integration, stating that he would support either separation or integration if it would bring about peace. He emphasized the importance of freedom, justice, and equality and denounced any form of bondage or oppression. Interestingly, Ali's words parallel the sentiments expressed by Abraham Lincoln during his time as the President of the United States. While Lincoln addressed physical slavery, Ali spoke about the emotional bondage and the need for a society that upholds freedom, justice, and equality. Both men shared a vision of a peaceful society and recognized the inherent conflict in a nation divided on fundamental issues. Ali's willingness to work toward peace and justice, regardless of the means, resonates with Lincoln's approach. Lincoln famously stated that he would save the Union by any means necessary, whether it involved freeing all slaves, freeing some while leaving others in bondage, or not freeing any.

Similarly, Ali focused on achieving peace and justice, understanding that the divided state of America in the 1960s mirrored the antebellum era when a divided nation faced the threat of collapse. At his core, Ali was driven by a longing for a society free of injustice and discrimination, and he advocated for working together with people of all races to achieve that goal. His humanitarian spirit was evident throughout his public life, even during a period marked by the contentious atmosphere of the 1960s and his association with the Nation of Islam.

Thomas Hauser, his chief biographer, and close friend, acknowledges Ali's evolution as a public figure and his changing views on social issues. Hauser emphasizes that Ali's mentality was not fixed, and he adapted to the changing times of his generation. During the tumultuous 1960s, Ali became a symbol of dissent in America, advocating for black pride and resistance against white domination. However, Hauser notes that not everything Ali preached during that time was wise, and Ali himself later rejected some of the beliefs he once adhered to. Growing up in the segregated South and experiencing the harsh realities of racism firsthand, Ali's perspective on race issues in

America was deeply influenced. As he traveled and gained recognition in boxing, he encountered racial injustices in various forms, further shaping his understanding of the ongoing struggle for equality. Ali believed in confronting racism directly and actively rather than adopting the passive approach of the civil rights movement. Despite his association with the Nation of Islam and his alignment with Elijah Muhammad, Ali did not wholeheartedly embrace the belief preached by Muhammad that all white people were devils. It is clear from Ali's rhetoric that he did not fully endorse or value such rhetoric, suggesting that his views on race were more nuanced and complex. Ali's statements in a May 1965 interview with Sports Illustrated's Jack Olsen provide a more practical depiction of where he stood:

> *You got to love your own kind. I just love my people and their children. I hug little Negro children when they come around the yard. They're so humble and sweet, and they don't bother nobody. They don't have a future, and nobody really teaches 'em the truth. I couldn't feel the same way about a white child 'cause he's not my kind, and then later, when he gets*

bigger, he'll have to turn away from me or else give up everything he's got just to be with some poor Negro. He's got brothers and sisters and friends that'd condemn him for being with me. Kennedy got killed. Lincoln got killed. They mean right, but they were surrounded by the other whites.

Ali's adept transition and control of the shifting rhetoric of the reactionary 1960s to the changes of the 1970s demonstrates Ali's astute awareness of societal shifts. Essentially, Ali recreated himself in response to the turbulence of the time.

CHAPTER SIX

MUHAMMAD ALI AND THE WAR IN VIETNAM

Ali's burgeoning fame and global popularity coincided with the highly controversial Vietnam War. However, he couldn't have foreseen the pivotal role he would play in the domestic politics surrounding the conflict. Speculation arose in the mid-1960s that Ali would be drafted into the military, fueling the rumors. In 1966, he was officially "reclassified 1-A," making him eligible for military service. While some government officials believed that Ali's popularity could be harnessed to promote the war effort, Ali firmly rejected any involvement in the war due to his Islamic faith. As a conscientious objector, he questioned how he could take someone's life when he prayed for peace five times daily. Beyond his religious convictions, Ali challenged the justification for the war, briefly stating, "I ain't got no quarrel with them

Vietcong." He then made the venomous statement that enraged the US government: "No Vietcong Ever Called Me Nigger." Ali did not want to engage in a conflict he could not ethically justify, whether for religious or social reasons:

> *Why should they ask me to put on a uniform and go ten thousand miles from home and drop bombs and bullets on brown people in Vietnam while so-called Negro people in Louisville are treated like dogs? If I thought going to war would bring freedom and equality to twenty-two million of my people, they wouldn't have to draft me. I'd join you tomorrow. But I either have to obey the laws of the land or the laws of Allah. I have nothing to lose by standing up and following my beliefs. We've been in jail for four hundred years.*

Ali's philosophical stance led him to reject participation in what he deemed an unjust war, whether it meant fighting abroad or serving in a symbolic role within the United States. Despite the severe consequences that followed, he stood firm in his principles. Stokely Carmichael observed that Ali's principled stand against the war made him the target of intense vilification and became the most hated black man in white America. While facing backlash from the white establishment, Ali became a source of inspiration for African Americans disproportionately affected by the Vietnam War. Gerald Early, a prominent professor, and author, vividly recalled the emotional impact of Ali's refusal to be drafted, seeing it as a defense of his honor as a black person and a human being. Soon, Ali was embroiled in a legal battle that jeopardized his boxing career and personal freedom. He was stripped of his title, suspended his boxing license, and sentenced to five years in prison on June 20, 1967. Although he was released on bail pending an appeal, his ban from boxing in the United States endured for over three years, and the revocation of his passport prevented him from competing internationally.

Ali's profound impact on the internal politics of the Vietnam War cannot be understated. He provided substantial support to an emerging anti-war movement. Julian Bond expressed astonishment at the level of political influence a sports figure like Ali could wield, emphasizing the breadth of his sphere of influence. By 1967, it became evident that Ali's reach extended beyond sports, leaving a significant imprint on various aspects of society. Ali's unwillingness to join the military made international headlines. African blacks, Asian Muslims, and European anti-Vietnam War protesters noted his stance. He steadfastly maintained his position, claiming a foundation of moral convictions. In doing so, Ali distributed a press release declaring:

> *It is in light of my own personal convictions that I take my stand in rejecting the call to be inducted into the armed services. I do so with full realization of its implications and possible consequences. I have searched my conscience and find I cannot be true to my belief in my religion by accepting such a call . . . . If justice prevails if my constitutional rights are upheld, I will be forced to go neither to the Army nor jail. In the end, I am confident that justice will come my way, for the truth must eventually prevail.*

This was a watershed moment for Ali because he was clearly no longer just a boxing champion but also a people's champion, a moniker he would bear for the rest of his life. He was willing to forego the best years of his boxing career as well as millions of dollars to champion a cause that energized America's left:

> *I was stopped right in my prime just when I started making money. . . . Tomorrow, I can go back to get the money if I would only deny my faith if I would only join up against my religion, I could easily go back to making millions. . . . I turned it down, and I go out still with my head high. . . . I'm not what they call an "Uncle Tom." . . . The flesh and the blood and the freedom of my people come before money.*

The impact of this period in Ali's boxing career was so significant that his longtime doctor, Ferdie Pacheco, lamented the world's loss, comparing it to the censorship of a Mozart symphony or a play by Shakespeare. Angelo Dundee echoed this sentiment, emphasizing that Ali's beliefs had deprived him of the best years of his life, a subject that should never be forgotten. Ali consciously decided to forgo wealth and fame within the boxing ring for a higher cause, passing on the prime of his career. Despite facing harsh criticism, he remained steadfast in his fight.

However, the most significant backlash Ali encountered was his refusal to comply with the Vietnam War draft policy. His popularity and controversial nature made him a polarizing figure at a time when the government sought to rally support for the increasingly contentious war. Ali fearlessly expressed his opposition to the war on national broadcasts, boldly stating his refusal to participate in a conflict that he believed perpetuated the domination of white slave masters over oppressed people. Critics in the media attacked Ali, accusing him of being anti-American and lacking patriotism. Producer and television personality David Susskind even went so far as to rebuke Ali directly on a talk show, denouncing him as a disgrace to his country, race, and profession. Despite the onslaught of insults, Ali maintained his dignity while those aligned with the establishment grew weary and distanced themselves from the former champion.

The denigration of Ali extended to the government as well. Congressman Frank Clark of Pennsylvania expressed his dismay at Ali's defiance of the war, urging citizens to boycott his performances. Maine Governor John Reed, who had been assisting in scheduling an upcoming Ali fight, changed his stance and deemed Ali deserving of contempt from patriotic Americans. Congressman Joe Waggonner of Louisiana, a World War II veteran, and segregationist, dismissed Ali as a phony. Even California Governor Ronald Reagan refused Ali a boxing license, calling him a draft-dodger. The criticism against Ali was not limited to politicians. Sportswriter Red Smith compared him to unpatriotic war protesters, while Jim Murray of the Los Angeles Times called him "the white man's burden." Even President Richard Nixon considered Ali his "pet peeve," according to Jackie Robinson. Ali began to face disapproval from prominent African Americans, including Robinson, who admired Ali as a fighting champion but criticized his desire to reap the benefits of the country while refusing to fight for it. Robinson believed that Ali's stance demoralized young black soldiers in Vietnam. Former boxing champion and military veteran Joe Louis also condemned Ali for his refusal to serve, stating that someone who doesn't want to fight for their country shouldn't have the honor of being a champion. Despite facing heavy criticism and losing support from some influential figures, Ali remained resilient and unwavering in his decision. He proudly asserted that he had lost nothing, having gained the respect of thousands worldwide and peace of mind.

The debate and attention surrounding Ali's conviction extended beyond the confines of the government. It was felt all throughout the world. "I can't take part in anything where I'd help the shooting of dark Asiatic people who haven't lynched me, deprived me of my freedom, justice, and equality, or assassinated my leaders," Ali concluded. Ali's anger shook America's elite and energized the left. Ali galvanized the anti-war movement and instilled tremendous black pride in his followers. During an interview on Stewart Thomas' talk show, "Say Brother," two years into his suspension, Ali stated emphatically, "I just don't think I should go ten thousand miles from here and shoot some black people who never called me nigger, never." During an interview on Stewart Thomas' talk show, "Say Brother," two years into his suspension, Ali stated emphatically: "I just don't think I should go ten thousand miles from here and shoot some black people who never called me nigger, never lynched me, never put dogs on me, never raped my mama, [for people who] enslaved me and deprived me of freedom, justice, [and] equality... I just can't shoot them." I can't go over there and shoot those people and then return home and be a nigger." The direct poignancy of Ali's words was crucial to his influence. No one in American history had openly confronted racism with such a huge audience.

Noam Chomsky, the renowned linguist from M.I.T., commended the profound simplicity of Ali's powerful statement, "I ain't got no quarrel with them Vietcong." This straightforward declaration struck a chord with people from diverse backgrounds because of its clarity. Chomsky emphasized that the statement raised critical questions about why underprivileged individuals in the United States were being coerced by wealthy individuals in the United States to kill impoverished individuals in Vietnam. Ali distilled a complex issue into understandable terms, resonating with many people. Once again, Ali demonstrated his ability to connect with a broad audience through the compelling power of his rhetoric.

Furthermore, the eccentric author Hunter S. Thompson was captivated by Ali's remark that "No

Vietcong ever called me Nigger." "Muhammad Ali said that, back in 1967, and he almost went to prison for it, which says all that needs to be said right now about justice & gibberish in the White House," Thompson reflected in 1978. "Ali decided one day a long time ago, not long after his twenty-first birthday, that he would be King of the World on his own turf and Crown Prince on everybody else's. Ali's brilliance was in both his words and actions because, in its purest form, the act of not fighting in what many worldwide believed was a kind of terrorism. Ali's brilliance was evident in his words and actions because, in its purest form, not participating in what many worldwide considered an unjustifiable war was universally admired. Ali's rejection of the Vietnam War lost him his professional boxing career, but his attitude had a lasting impact on his personal legacy.

Ali's sensibility carried him even more into the world's good graces. While America's conservative base despised him for his opposition to the war, the country's growing antiwar movement hailed Ali as a hero. The foresight of prominent philosopher and Ali friend Lord Bertrand Russell, who encouraged him during the height of the criticism not to worry too much about the consequences: "The air will shift. "I have a feeling." To that end, Eduardo Galeano, a prominent South American writer, accurately portrayed the impact of Ali's refusal to be conscripted and subsequent conviction in his poem, Ali:

> *He was a butterfly and a bee. In the ring, he floated and stung. In 1967, Muhammad Ali, born Cassius Clay, refused to put on a uniform. 'Got nothing against no Viet Cong,' He said. 'Ain't no Vietnamese ever called me nigger.' They called him a traitor. They sentenced him to a five-year jail term and barred him from boxing. They stripped him of his title as champion of the world. The punishment became his trophy. By taking away his crown, they anointed him king. Years later, a few college students asked him to recite something. And for them, he improvised the shortest poem in world literature: 'Me, we.'*

Galeano's tribute to Ali is remarkably powerful. His assertion that the government's punishment of Ali elevated him to a "king" is a sharp and poignant characterization, particularly considering that Ali had been proclaiming himself as such since his victory over Liston in 1964. Indeed, Ali's enduring legacy and global fame were greatly enhanced by his personal sacrifices and courageous stance on the Vietnam War. Throughout his ordeal, Ali reassured his followers that he was doing fine and that his commitment to humanitarianism and leadership remained unwavering. He stated, "To those who believe I lost so much by not taking that step, I haven't lost a thing. I have gained a great deal. Firstly, I have gained peace of mind. I have gained a piece of my heart. I now know that I am content with almighty God himself." This mindset served as a guiding force for Ali during his three-and-a-half-year absence from boxing. During this period, Ali's popularity skyrocketed. He became a cultural icon and symbol for the two major struggles of the era: the civil rights movement and the Vietnam War. Ali's involvement in the anti-war movement transformed him into a figure of immense significance. He was no longer solely a boxer with strong views on race and religion. As the already divisive war raged on, Ali became even more entangled in the tumultuous issues of the 1960s. He fearlessly expressed his beliefs while embarking on a nationwide speaking tour that took him from one coast to another.

In doing so, Ali refused to accept criticism from the old white establishment. Rather than adjusting his attitude, Ali continued antagonizing a power system that had treated blacks indignantly during the war effort. "I was determined to be one nigger that the white man didn't get," Ali said. One nigger you didn't catch, white man. Do you get it? You're not going to get one nigger. You're not going to get one nigger." Historian Randy Roberts perfectly described Ali's legacy regarding race and war: "Ali became the people's champion, a folk hero for liberals and an antihero for conservatives."

Ali became a living symbol, representing the struggles of black Americans and the opposition to the Vietnam War. By the time the Supreme Court overturned his draft conviction, he had transcended sports to become the most globally recognized and politically influential athlete in history. Throughout his boxing career, Ali was a powerful voice for the people, advocating for those facing oppression, despair, and injustice worldwide. The hope and inspiration that Ali embodied during the Vietnam era were unparalleled. Other great athletes of the time, including Kareem Abdul-Jabbar, Bill Russell, and Jim Brown, followed Ali's lead in using their platforms to drive positive change on social issues. However, they all recognized Ali as their foremost leader. Abdul-Jabbar stated that Ali didn't need their support because he already had the heart of the black community and gave countless people the courage to challenge the system. Similarly, Bill Russell emphasized that Ali was truly free at a time when freedom was incredibly challenging to attain, regardless of one's background or status. Ali's embodiment of freedom served as a model that instilled hope for a better future among African Americans and played a significant role in advancing black history.

Even as the Vietnam War drew to a close in the mid-1970s, Ali wanted to emphasize that his opposition to the war and refusal to be drafted did not make him anti-American. He made it clear that his stance was based on moral grounds. In 1975, Ali expressed that he would have been willing to fight in a war with a justifiable purpose but not in a war that he considered unjust. He stated that if America were under attack and facing foreign forces, he would fight to protect himself, his children, and his people. He believed that if black people were armed, it would deter violence from foreign invaders. Ali's patriotism, however, was never fully appreciated by the conservative establishment. His critics, particularly those who opposed his decision not to serve in the military, never forgave him. In recent years, there have been instances where Ali's honorary celebrations faced backlash due to his association with the Vietnam War. For example, during the 2004 Major League Baseball All-Star game, fellow honoree and World War II veteran Bob Feller strongly objected to Ali's presence, citing his name change and religious conversion as evasive tactics to avoid serving his country. Feller believed that one should serve their country regardless of personal circumstances. However, Feller misunderstood the reasons behind Ali's name change and religious affiliation. The underlying point is that some Americans never forgave Ali for his opposition to the Vietnam War, despite his unwavering commitment to his beliefs.

CHAPTER SEVEN

THE RETURN OF THE KING

Ali returned to boxing on October 26, 1970, against Jerry Quarry. The quarry was a vivacious twenty-five-year-old who became one of boxing's most popular combatants during Ali's exile. The bout occurred in Atlanta, but spectators worldwide tuned in to watch Ali's comeback. On the day of the fight, Reverend Jesse Jackson talked to George Plimpton and stated:

Symbolically, [if Ali loses], it would suggest that the forces of blind patriotism are right, that dissent is wrong, that protest means you don't love the country . . . . They tried to railroad him. They refused to believe his testimony about his convictions and his religion. They wouldn't let him practice his profession. They tried to break his spirit and his body. Martin Luther King has a song: 'Truth crushed to the earth will rise again.' That's the black ethos. With [Ali], all we had was the hope, the psychological longing for his return. And it happened! In Georgia, of all places, and against a white man. . . . So there are tremendous social implications. [Ali's] a hero.

The location of the fight in Atlanta, where segregationist views were prevalent, added an undeniable sense of drama to the event. Governor Lester Maddox of Georgia attempted to halt the fight, considering it a tragic occurrence that Ali would make his return to the state. He expressed disbelief that a fight featuring a man who had denounced his country's uniform and refused induction could occur anywhere in the United States. Eminent boxing commentator Bert Sugar astutely captured the moment's significance, recognizing the symbolism inherent in the setting. He described the Ali-Quarry fight in Atlanta as a gathering of unprecedented black financial power and influence, a striking contrast to the historical backdrop of the Old Confederacy. People from various factions of the civil rights movement came together to witness the event, demonstrating their unwavering support for Ali. The fight captivated the audience, and Ali swiftly defeated Quarry in the third round. Coretta Scott King, the wife of Martin Luther King Jr., commended Ali after the fight, acknowledging him not only as a boxing champion but also as a champion of justice, peace, and human dignity. The Quarry fight marked the beginning of Ali's eager return to the boxing spotlight, as he remained uncertain about his future for his boxing career. He was acutely aware that his boxing privileges could be revoked again soon.

Despite concerns about his readiness, Ali fought against Oscar Bonavena of Argentina just two months after his December return. It was a grueling fifteen-round battle, but Ali emerged victorious, maintaining his undefeated professional record. His doctor, Ferdie Pacheco, believed Ali had endured significant punishment in defeating Bonavena. After his lengthy hiatus from the sport, he questioned whether he was truly prepared to face the champion, Joe Frazier. However, the allure of the money and the uncertainty of Ali's future led him to pursue the opportunity. Ali wasted no time in launching a verbal assault on Frazier, and within three months, they faced each other in the ring. The fight between Ali and Frazier on March 8, 1971, at Madison Square Garden in New York City was a highly anticipated spectacle. The "Fight of the Century" is widely regarded as one of the greatest fights in boxing history. Ali playfully remarked on the worldwide anticipation, humorously suggesting that countries around the globe would pause for the event. Ali had transformed into a fighter and a cultural icon, attracting a massive following from all corners of the world.

Conversely, he belittled Frazier, considering him unintelligent and undeserving of support. The pre-fight rhetoric, largely influenced by pro-Vietnam sentiments, portrayed Frazier as aligned with white conservatives, while Ali was positioned as the embodiment of black America. In some instances, Frazier was even labeled the "Great White Hope," a role ironically thrust upon him despite his own experiences representing the black community and its struggles in America.

Joe Frazier's upbringing in Beaufort, South Carolina, was marked by poverty. He was one of thirteen children and did not receive an education beyond the ninth grade. Frazier was not politically inclined, and his deprived background reflected the challenges faced by black individuals in the South following years of slavery. However, due to Ali's relentless verbal attacks, Frazier was unjustly labeled as an "Uncle Tom." Bryant Gumbel, an intellectual commentator, noted that Frazier became a symbol that those who despised Ali could rally behind. Frazier's unfortunate role in the Ali-Frazier rivalry overshadowed his struggle and the representation of the black man's plight. Gumbel expressed regret that Frazier never received the recognition he deserved as a man. Ali's treatment of Frazier was undeniably disrespectful, as he demeaned him personally and publicly. With hindsight, Ali came to regret his actions and the personal attacks he launched against Frazier. Frazier's manager, Dave Wolf, described Ali's treatment as cruel, highlighting that Frazier, based on his background and upbringing, embodied the qualities Ali claimed to be fighting for. Ali's behavior went beyond what was necessary, with moments that deeply hurt Frazier and left a lasting impact. Some of Ali's actions seemed calculated to gain a psychological edge in the fight, but they extended far beyond that purpose. There was a bullying and sadistic quality to Ali's behavior, akin to tormenting a vulnerable creature. This portrayal of Ali during his rivalry with Frazier is certainly not one of his finest moments, and critics have rightly condemned his use of verbal prowess in such a terrible manner. In his later years, Ali expressed remorse for the hurtful relationship he had created with Frazier.

Frazier's victory over Ali in their epic fifteen-round clash sent shockwaves through the boxing world. Despite being hurt badly during the fight, Ali showed his resilience and determination by finishing the match on his feet. The Hong Kong Standard described Ali's refusal to stay down as a testament to his pride, athleticism, and warrior spirit. It was the first loss of Ali's professional career, but even in defeat, he became immortalized. The impact of Ali's loss went beyond the realm of sports. The defeat deeply affected Bryant Gumbel, among many other African Americans. Gumbel expressed that the tears he shed were not just for Ali's loss in the boxing ring but because Ali symbolized so much more. Ali represented wars, race, politics, society, and generations. The sentiment among many was that if

Ali lost, they were wrong in their beliefs and hopes. Grief and depression were felt by people all over the world. Ali, however, tried to downplay the significance of the loss, emphasizing that there were more important things to worry about in life. Nonetheless, the impact of Ali's defeat was profound.

Ambalavaner Sivanandan, a Sri Lankan writer dedicated himself to improving race relations, expressed his sorrow by recognizing Ali's larger role as a humanitarian. He saw Ali's passing as a moment where the black world mourned the loss of their king but also recognized that Ali's legacy would inspire every black man to become his own king. Sivanandan noted that Ali represented the release of the black athlete from the confines of the civil rights movement and into the realm of broader liberation. This perspective unsettled white society because Ali was not just a prizefighter but a symbol of black empowerment in its many forms. Indeed, Sivanandan's words captured the sentiments of many black people worldwide during that time in 1971. Muhammad Ali's fame and influence were unparalleled, and he became a global icon for freedom and justice for the underrepresented. On June 28,

1971, four years after his conviction and shortly after his fight with Frazier, the Supreme Court overturned Ali's sentence on a technicality, dismissing all charges against him. This ruling freed Ali to resume his quest to regain his championship. He participated in fourteen fights over the next three years, including a victory over Frazier in January 1974. During this period, Ali traveled extensively, further solidifying his status as a cultural figure and a spokesperson on a global scale. One of the most significant events in Ali's career was the fight against George Foreman, which took place in Kinshasa, Zaire. This monumental international event was the setting for Ali's attempt to reclaim the championship. Ali felt at home in this environment and embraced the opportunity to showcase his skills and message to the world.

The "Rumble in the Jungle" against George Foreman on October 30, 1974, was a highly anticipated event that showcased the prevailing sense of Pan-Africanism. Ali capitalized on this sentiment and garnered overwhelming support from black communities in America and Africa. Norman Mailer, who closely followed Ali during his time in Zaire, documented Ali's cultural advantage in his book "The

Fight." According to Mailer's account, the people of Zaire revered Ali as a god-like figure. Much like Frazier, Foreman was portrayed as the adversary, almost representing the white establishment or a black man fighting on behalf of whites to suppress Ali's voice and status. The intensity and excitement surrounding the fight resonated deeply with black people worldwide. Stokely Carmichael, reflecting on the significance of Ali to his generation, described him as a "warrior saint" and praised his moral courage, principles, and love for his people. In Zaire, Ali's following was immense. He was mobbed by supporters wherever he went, attracting people of all ages and genders who admired him for his athletic prowess, moral stance, and sacrifices made in the name of principle. The fight against Foreman became a powerful symbol of defiance and triumph for black communities, reinforcing Ali's role as a global icon for justice and empowerment.

The political dynamics between fight promoters and the corrupt dictator King Mobutu Sese Seko in Zaire during the "Rumble in the Jungle" were complex and troubling. Mobutu was known for running a kleptocracy, where he amassed immense wealth while the average citizen of Zaire lived in extreme poverty, with an annual income of approximately seventy dollars. Despite the disturbing reality of Mobutu's regime, Ali's work and impact in Africa during that time remain noteworthy. The documentary "When We Were Kings" by Leon Gast captures the significance of Ali's presence in the African community. Africans would gather around Ali during his training sessions, chanting in unison, "Ali Bomaye, Ali Bomaye!" which translates to "Ali, kill him!" This demonstrates the immense support and admiration Ali received from the African masses. Ferdie Pacheco, Ali's doctor, recalled the awe-inspiring scenes of Ali's interactions with the people of Zaire. Even in areas without basic amenities like electricity or television, everyone recognized and loved Ali. His power over the people and the love they showed him were truly remarkable. The documentary footage of Ali among the crowds in Zaire evokes strong emotions. However, Foreman did not enjoy a significant following in Zaire, highlighting the contrast in popularity and support between the two fighters during their time in Africa.

The overwhelming favorability of Muhammad Ali among Africans during the "Rumble in the Jungle" was a testament to his magnetism and the genuine connection he established with people. Despite George Foreman's physical resemblance to native Africans, he was perplexed and disturbed by the African crowd's emotional reaction, feeling alienated compared to Ali. One native of Zaire expressed the sentiment shared by many Africans, stating that they were all for Muhammad Ali because he was seen as a genuine and authentic person defending a righteous cause, not simply based on his physical appearance. They recognized Ali's commitment to Africa, his support for the African liberation movements, and his worldwide advocacy for justice and equality. Norman Mailer, in his account, noted the irony in the situation. Although Foreman appeared to be more "black" regarding physical features, Ali, with his mixed heritage, had certain aspects of his personality that seemed to reflect a "whiteness" associated with a confident, charismatic figure. Mailer described Ali's contradictions and complexities, highlighting the various dimensions of his identity. Nevertheless, the rallying cry of "Ali, Bomaye" ("Ali, kill him") resonated throughout Kinshasa, and Ali demonstrated remarkable control over the masses. His ability to connect with people, inspire devotion and mobilize support showcased his exceptional charisma and public appeal.

Muhammad Ali was thrilled about the opportunity to fight in Zaire, and he proudly expressed his admiration for the country and its predominantly black population. He emphasized the significance of a country operated by black people, where black soldiers, the president, and the faces on the currency were all black. Ali wished that all black people in America could witness this experience and feel the empowerment it brought. The fight in Zaire was seen as a symbol of black pride and empowerment. Government signs proclaimed it a fight between two black men in a black nation, organized and witnessed by the world. Ali's enthusiasm for the fight was evident in his poetic declarations, comparing his victory over George Foreman to the shock of Richard Nixon's resignation. Despite Ali's spirited confidence, many doubted his ability to defeat Foreman, considering him an older and slower boxer at that point in his career. Foreman was favored at three-to-one odds, and even announcer Howard Cosell expressed concern, suggesting it might be time to bid farewell to Ali. However, Ali responded playfully, citing his wife's comment about Cosell's decline, indicating that he still had the skills and determination to prevail. Drawing parallels to his historic victory over Sonny Liston, Ali declared that Foreman would suffer the same fate. He exuded his signature bravado, expressing certainty that he would become the champion again, proclaiming himself to be fighting another Sonny Liston.

While Muhammad Ali projected confidence and bravado, many believe he harbored an underlying fear, particularly when facing George Foreman. Foreman had convincingly defeated Joe Frazier and Ken Norton, who had previously defeated Ali. He was widely regarded as the most feared heavyweight boxer in the world at that time. There was a prevalent belief among boxing correspondents that Ali was no longer the same fighter he had been in his twenties. During the three years following his exile from the sport for refusing to join the army, Ali had engaged in various activities, such as lecturing, acting on stage in New York, and traveling, leading some to question his focus and readiness as a fighter. Similar to the concerns raised before Ali's fight against Sonny Liston a decade earlier, albeit for different reasons, people felt that Ali was in danger against Foreman. Even Henry Clark, a talented heavyweight boxer who sparred with Foreman and was a friend of Ali's, expressed apprehension about the punishing power of Foreman's punches. Clark believed that Ali might risk getting hurt, as Foreman was exceptionally punishing in his blows. Nevertheless, Ali responded to his critics uniquely, rebuking their doubts and guaranteeing a victory with his customary flair and poetic expression.

Muhammad Ali viewed the fight against George Foreman in Zaire as more than just a boxing match. For him, it was an opportunity to continue his mission of promoting social justice and effecting global change. While winning boxing matches held significance, Ali saw the sport as a means to achieve broader goals and convey important messages. Ali recognized that his position as a fighter provided him with a platform to address and raise awareness about issues that he deemed crucial. He understood that boxing could serve as a vehicle for him to convey certain points and provoke discussions that might not have been possible without his involvement in the sport. His ultimate aim was not merely to seek personal glory in the ring but to bring about tangible change in various aspects of society. By leveraging his status as a prominent boxer and charismatic figure, Ali used his platform to promote humanitarian causes, advocate for social justice, and challenge prevailing norms and prejudices. He saw boxing as a tool to amplify his voice and positively impact the world beyond the realm of sports. Ali's actual perspective of the fight's significance was magnificently portrayed in an interview with legendary British broadcaster David Frost just before the fight:

> *I'm representing the freedom of black people in America. I want to be the one black man who stands up and look[s] at white people and tell[s] the truth, who don't sell 'em out, who don't Uncle Tom. . . . [who] take[s] his fame to uplift his little brother in the ghetto. . . . [Other famous blacks] are white minded . . . they don't think black . . . they get their fame, and they leave their little people . . . I wanna win so I can come home and speak for the brother who's living in [a] rat-infested house, sleeping on concrete in the ghetto . . . so, God, I'm your tool, I'm your servant, let me get this man tonight! . . .*

This is the way I feel. So, I'm not fighting for me.
. . . I'm fighting slavery.

Muhammad Ali's impact and influence went beyond the boxing ring. He understood his role's significance and power as symbolizing black pride and social change. His interviews and interactions with figures like David Frost showcased the emotional depth and admiration people felt toward him. His extensive travels and interactions with diverse communities shaped Ali's understanding of his global significance. He recognized that he represented the black population in America and people worldwide who looked up to him. With a victory over Foreman, Ali saw an opportunity to promote the causes he believed in and become a prominent advocate for social change. Ali's audacious nature and glorious vision of himself as a world leader amazed many, including Norman Mailer. He defied expectations and stereotypes, rising above the role society might have assigned him. Ali's charismatic rhetoric and bold predictions captivated the press and his followers, creating an atmosphere of excitement and anticipation leading up to the fight. Ali's confident proclamations about the upcoming fight reflected his belief in his own abilities and the impact he could make. He saw the fight against Foreman as an opportunity for a historic upset that would reverberate beyond the boxing world and be perceived as a monumental achievement and a miraculous event. Overall, Muhammad Ali's influence extended far beyond the boundaries of boxing, and he used his platform to champion social causes and inspire people worldwide. His larger-than-life persona and ability to captivate audiences with his words and actions made him a cultural icon and a symbol of hope and empowerment.

The atmosphere in Kinshasa before the fight between Ali and Foreman was tense and filled with anticipation. The fight was scheduled to accommodate the viewing audience in the United States, starting at four o'clock in the morning local time. Despite the early hour, the setting in Kinshasa was vibrant and penetrating. Norman Mailer, who was with Ali's team in the hours leading up to the fight, described the atmosphere in Ali's dressing room as surreal. The mood was somber, with a sense of impending doom. Many believed that Ali would be defeated and subjected to a severe beating from Foreman. Ali's team's fear and anxiety were palpable, as they genuinely worried about his well-being. However, Ali, ever the showman and master of rhetoric, felt the need to uplift his team's spirits. He questioned why everyone was so unhappy and then exclaimed, "I'm gonna dance!" His statement had a powerful effect, and the whole team began to scream that they would dance. It was a testament to Ali's ability to influence and inspire those around him, even in fear and doubt. Mailer marveled at the interaction, noting that Ali managed to lift their spirits and make them half-happy. With the resounding chants of "Ali, Bomaye!" ("Ali, kill him!") from the crowd, the fight commenced. The atmosphere was electric, reflecting the immense support and enthusiasm for Ali in Kinshasa.

In the fight against Foreman, Ali employed an unconventional strategy. He began the first round by throwing more right hands than usual, surprising Foreman and the spectators. He then transitioned into his famous "rope-a-dope" tactic, allowing Foreman to unleash a barrage of punches on him while he leaned against the ropes, aiming to tire out his opponent. Ferdie Pacheco, Ali's physician, and cornerman, described Ali's night performance as truly inspired. Ali showcased an incredible chin, courage, and ability to think creatively and clearly, even during a storm of punches. Pacheco considered it the most amazing performance he had ever witnessed. Ali's "rope-a-dope" strategy proved successful, and he pulled off one of the greatest upsets in boxing history. The people of Zaire erupted in jubilation, and David Frost, who was ringside, exclaimed the joyous scene and declared Ali, the winner. It was a moment of pure celebration and joy. The victory over Foreman was a redemption for Ali. It was seen as a reclaiming of the title that many believed had been unjustly taken away from him when he was stripped of his championship seven years earlier. The win elevated Ali's stature in the world, and even his critics couldn't deny the positive impact and goodwill generated by his triumph.

By reclaiming the title against Foreman, Ali had entered uncharted territory in his career. President Gerald Ford invited him to the White House less than two months after the fight to express his congratulations. Conservatives who had never forgiven Ali for refusing to submit to the draft were outraged, but President Ford insisted on pushing forward with the recall,

when I took office, we as a nation were pretty much torn apart. There were conflicts between families, in colleges, and on the streets. We'd gone through some serious race problems; the Vietnam War had heightened differences, and, of course, there was the heritage of Watergate. And one of the major challenges my administration faced was how we could heal the country. . . . I think that during the two-and-a-half years, I was president, we did that, and having Muhammad Ali come to the Oval Office was part of our overall effort. . . . he was a man of principle. I know there were some who thought he evaded his military responsibility, but I've never questioned anybody's dedication to whatever religion they believe in . . . . I accepted his decision. And because of his principles, I firmly believe that as time goes on, Muhammad Ali will be remembered for more than just excellence in athletics. I suppose it's premature to say how history will be written, but I'm sure *his page will talk about him as more than just a superb athlete.*

The third fight between Ali and Frazier, known as "The Thrilla in Manila," marked another significant moment in Ali's career. The fight, held in the Philippines on October 1, 1975, was highly anticipated and garnered an estimated seven hundred million viewers worldwide. The intense heat and humidity added to the grueling conditions of the match. True to his form, Ali engaged in a war of words with Frazier leading up to the fight, intensifying the personal feud between the two fighters. Frazier expressed his desire to defeat Ali and inflict pain upon him, stating, "I want to hurt him. I don't want to knock him out. I want to take his heart out." The fight itself was a brutal battle for both men. They traded powerful blows, enduring punishment and displaying tremendous resilience. The contest showcased the unwavering determination and indomitable spirit of both fighters. Ultimately, the fight stopped after the fourteenth round when Frazier's trainer, Eddie Futch, decided to throw in the towel, concerned for Frazier's well-being. Ali emerged as the victor, but the price paid by both men was evident. The fight took a significant toll on their physical and mental states. "The Thrilla in Manila" remains one of the most memorable and grueling matches in boxing history. It exemplified the fierce rivalry between Ali and Frazier, their unyielding determination, and the sacrifices they were willing to make to pursue victory.

The grueling nature of the fight took its toll on both Ali and Frazier. They relentlessly exchanged powerful blows throughout the match, pushing each other to their physical and mental limits. Witnesses, such as Associated Press writer Ed Schuyler, described it as a relentless battle where both fighters gave their all. Ferdie Pacheco, reflecting on the fight, remarked on the intensity and the mutual competitive edge and, at times, even hatred between Ali and Frazier. The fight seemed to reach a level where survival itself was in question. The harsh weather conditions in the Philippines compounded the physical strain on both fighters. Ali, in particular, felt the impact of the punishment and even expressed the feeling of being close to death in his corner. Angelo Dundee, his trainer, recalled Ali's statement about feeling like he was dying and equating it to what death must feel like. By the end of the fourteenth round, both fighters were exhausted and battered. It appeared unlikely that either of them could continue for the final round. Frazier's corner man, Eddie Futch, ended the fight to protect his fighter from further damage. Frazier protested, but Futch reassured him that his efforts in the fight would never be forgotten. The "Thrilla in Manila" left a lasting impact on both Ali and Frazier, physically and emotionally. It was a grueling battle showcasing their immense determination and will to win, but it highlighted the toll such fights can take on the human body.

In terrible pain, Ali later remarked, "My God, what that man did to me." Pacheco succinctly expressed Ali's devastation: "Ali was badly beaten up... he said that fight was the closest thing to death he knew of." Indeed, Ali was cited on the front page of the Washington Post the next day as declaring, "What you saw tonight was next to death." It is widely believed that the punishment Ali sustained in his fights, particularly against Frazier and Foreman, as well as his continued boxing career in the late 1970s and early 1980s, had a detrimental impact on his health. Many attribute his decline in health to the cumulative effects of the beatings he endured in the ring. The "Thrilla in Manila" against Frazier is often cited as a turning point in Ali's physical well-being. The brutal nature of the fight, combined with the intense heat and humidity, took a toll on both fighters. Ali's health reportedly deteriorated significantly after that match. Ali remained committed to using his voice to positively impact the world as his health declined. He continued to travel extensively and engage in humanitarian efforts, reaching out to those in need and championing various causes.

However, his boxing career ended somberly with fights against Larry Holmes in 1980 and Trevor Berbick in 1981, which ended in losses for Ali. It was evident that Ali was no longer in fighting shape, and doctors had advised against him participating in the Holmes fight. During the Holmes fight, Holmes himself pleaded with the referee to stop the match, recognizing the pounding Ali was enduring. Howard Cosell, the renowned sports commentator and longtime friend of Ali, also called for someone to intervene and end the fight due to the punishment Ali was sustaining. These later fights in Ali's career are often viewed with sadness and regret, as it became apparent that his health had declined to a point where he could no longer compete at his previous level. The toll of his boxing career, both physically and mentally, was evident, and the circumstances surrounding those fights raised concerns about his well-being.

Barack Obama's remarks at Ali's funeral in 2016 effectively captured the range of emotions that the Holmes bout evoked in black Americans:

> *It was 1980, and an epic career was in its twilight. Everybody knew it, probably including The Champ himself. Ali went into one of his final fights as an underdog; all the smart money was on the new champ, Larry Holmes. And in the end, the odds makers were right. A few hours later, at 4 a.m., after the loss, after all the fans had gone, a sportswriter asked a restroom attendant if he'd bet on the fight. The man— black, getting on in years—said he'd put his money on Ali. The writer asked why. 'Why?' he said. 'Why? Because he's Muhammad Ali, that's why. Mister, I'm 72 years old. I owe the man for giving me my dignity.'*

Ali was a shell of the fighter he once was, but he couldn't stop himself from putting on a show for his millions of fans and using boxing as a platform to preach kindness. He realized he should have retired as early as 1977, when he told an audience in Newcastle, England:

I want to retire after [my next fight], but . . . I talked to about twenty African presidents and a couple of those who are fighting for independence . . . and I'm so surprised to find out that every one of those presidents knew me, they knew my history, and they all want me to come to their country, and all their people want me to come to their country. And I found out that through boxing, I can do so much to help so many people. And our people in the states. And for me to give up and to get out of the public . . . at this time when the world is struggling, and there's so much I can do would be terrible. And through boxing . . . there's so much I can do . . . I want to do something to help humanity.

Indeed, after his boxing career ended, Muhammad Ali faced the challenge of Parkinson's disease, which gradually affected his physical abilities, including his renowned ability to speak. Despite the difficulties posed by the disease, Ali remained committed to positively impacting the world and continued to be an influential figure. Although his verbal communication was diminished, Ali found alternative ways to contribute and inspire. He became a global ambassador for peace, humanitarianism, and social justice. He traveled extensively, met with world leaders, and engaged in various charitable endeavors. Ali used his fame and influence to raise awareness about important issues, such as civil rights, racial equality, religious tolerance, and humanitarian causes. Even as his physical condition deteriorated, Ali's spirit remained strong, and he continued to inspire and touch people's lives worldwide. His legacy extended beyond his boxing achievements, as he became a symbol of resilience, courage, and the power of determination. Throughout the last three decades of his life, Ali's positive impact on society persisted. He was a role model for many, showing that one's influence and ability to make a difference can extend far beyond their prime years. Ali's commitment to social justice and his unwavering spirit resonate and inspire others today.

CHAPTER EIGHT

LIFE AFTER BOXING

Muhammad Ali's post-boxing life showcased his remarkable character and commitment to promoting peace, understanding, and forgiveness. Despite his battle with Parkinson's disease, Ali remained dedicated to his role as a global ambassador and used his platform to spread messages of unity and forgiveness. Ali's retirement allowed him to delve deeper into his spiritual journey, emphasizing the importance of inner growth and self-reflection. He recognized that his true work began after his boxing career, indicating that his impact on the world extended far beyond the ring. Ali's ability to transcend boundaries and connect with people from all walks of life was a testament to his universal appeal. He became a symbol of goodwill and inspiration, transcending continents, languages, colors, and oceans. His journey from being a polarizing figure to a beloved international treasure demonstrated the power of transformation and the capacity for individuals to change and grow. Ali's belief in forgiveness was a central theme in his life. Despite facing persecution and hardship, he chose not to seek revenge against those who hurt him. Instead, he practiced forgiveness and encouraged others to do the same. His ability to forgive showcased his character strength and commitment to promoting peace and understanding. Muhammad Ali's legacy as a world hero lies in his accomplishments as a boxer and his unwavering dedication to spreading love, compassion, and unity. His impact on society continues to inspire generations, reminding us of the power of forgiveness, the pursuit of peace, and the ability of one individual to make a lasting difference in the world.

Muhammad Ali's impact extended beyond boxing, inspiring individuals such as Nelson Mandela, who saw him as heroic. Mandela recognized Ali's courage and commitment, making him his personal hero and inspiring millions of young, black South Africans. Even during Mandela's imprisonment, he drew strength from Ali's example. In the later years of

Ali's life, as his health declined and his rhetorical abilities were diminished, he focused on healing and fostering positive interactions between people worldwide. Despite his fame and success in boxing, Ali remained aware of the complex nature of his chosen profession. He grappled with the idea that boxing, a sport where black men engaged in physical combat for entertainment, was the platform through which he challenged and confronted white society. Ali's conflicted feelings about boxing highlight his understanding of the systemic issues and inequalities that existed in society. He recognized that boxing provided him with a platform to advocate for social change, but he also questioned the underlying dynamics of the sport. Ali demonstrated a profound commitment to using his platform for the greater good through his actions. He used his influence and fame to bring attention to social justice issues, promote unity, and inspire others. Ali's ability to navigate these complexities and remain dedicated to his principles contributed to his enduring legacy as a symbol of courage, resilience, and the pursuit of justice. In 1970, Ali expressed his feelings of conflict by suggesting that he was still not respected by white society:

> [White people] stand around and say, 'Good fight, boy; you're a good boy; good goin.' They don't look at fighters as having brains. They don't look at fighters to be businessmen, humans, or intelligent. Fighters are just brutes that come to entertain the rich white people. Beat up on each other and break each other's noses, bleed, and show off like two little monkeys for the crowd, killing each other for the crowd. And half the crowd is white. We're just like two slaves in that ring. The masters get two of us big old black slaves and let us fight it out while they bet: 'My slave can whup your slave.' That's what I see when I see two black people fighting.

Muhammad Ali's understanding of the connection between boxing and the history of slavery was a profound aspect of his life. He recognized the violent origins of the sport but also understood how he could use it as a platform to shed light on the struggles African Americans faced during the Jim Crow era. For Ali, being an athlete went beyond sports; he saw it as an opportunity to bring about social change. Ali's contemporaries, like tennis star Arthur Ashe, recognized his pioneering role in combining athletic talent with social activism. Ashe acknowledged that Ali's impact extended far beyond his athletic achievements and made him an icon for millions of black Americans during a time when both Ali and the black social revolution were at their peak. Despite facing difficulties in formal education due to dyslexia, Ali possessed a unique intelligence and emotional competence that surpassed his peers. He may not have excelled in traditional academic settings. Still, his experiences traveling the world, interacting with diverse people, and immersing himself in different cultures gave him invaluable knowledge and insights. Ali's ability to absorb and share knowledge through his eloquence and charisma set him apart. Attempting to measure Ali's intelligence with a standard IQ test was considered inadequate by those who knew him well. His intellect and wisdom went beyond what could be quantified. Ali's ability to challenge white society through his words and actions made him one of the most recognizable figures globally. He harnessed his verbal eloquence to advocate for black people's rights and advancement and inspire unity and self-love within the community.

Ali's dedication to uplifting his community and fighting against the remnants of slavery persisted throughout his life. He urged black people to love themselves, support one another, and work towards positive change. These causes remained close to his heart until his passing in 2016, leaving a lasting legacy as a powerful advocate for justice and equality. Indeed, Muhammad Ali's journey and transformation throughout his life are widely revered and celebrated. The characterization of Ali in the 1960s, particularly when he was still known as Cassius Clay, differed from the man he became in later years. At twenty-two, Ali was known for his bold and outspoken nature, often advocating for the separation of blacks and whites as promoted by the Black Muslims. He aligned himself with the party-line of the Nation of Islam, which called for the separation of races to protect African Americans from the oppression of a racist system. During this period, Ali aimed to address what he perceived as social injustice in America. His outspokenness and firm stance on racial issues garnered positive and negative attention and contributed to his reputation as a controversial figure. His refusal to be drafted into the Vietnam War further solidified his position as a symbol of resistance and activism.

However, as Ali matured and his experiences broadened, his views and approach evolved. He embraced Sunni Islam in the late 1970s and distanced himself from the separatist ideology of the Nation of Islam. Ali's transformation was characterized by a shift towards a more inclusive and unifying message. He advocated for peace, love, and understanding among people of all races and backgrounds. In the latter part of the twentieth century and into the twenty-first century, Ali shifted towards promoting humanitarian causes, such as advocating for world peace, supporting charitable organizations, and working towards social justice. He became a global ambassador for goodwill, using his fame and platform to champion unity and compassion. It is the growth and evolution of Ali's beliefs and actions that have resonated deeply with people around the world. His journey from a young loudmouth to a global icon of peace and unity showcases the power of personal growth, introspection, and the willingness to challenge and transcend one's beliefs. Ali's legacy extends far beyond his accomplishments in the ring, as he continues to inspire generations with his commitment to positively impacting society. Ali knew his role in sport gave him the stage to affect change, and he relished the opportunity:

> *There were many ways for people to participate in the Civil Rights movement of the 1960s . . . . At the time, I chose to join the Nation of Islam, which promoted Black pride and independence . . . .Whatever approach you chose, the goal was the same: We all wanted freedom, justice, and equality for Black people in America. Martin Luther King Jr. made a difference. The NAACP made a difference. Rosa Parks made a difference. Malcolm X made a difference. Elijah Muhammad made a difference. I would like to think I made a difference, too.*

Muhammad Ali's journey of growth and transformation played a crucial role in shaping his noble standing and humanitarian appeal. While his language and confrontations with racism initially put him in a precarious position with mainstream America, it is through understanding his evolution over time that we can fully grasp how he achieved such a status. During the 1960s, Ali emerged as the most popular voice of his generation, alongside civil rights leader Martin Luther King Jr. His outspokenness and unapologetic stance against racism resonated deeply with black people across the country and the world. Ali's influence on black consciousness was profound, as he helped internationalize the struggle for racial equality. Despite his association with the Nation of Islam, a militant sect at the time, Ali's interpretation of Islam matured throughout the 1960s. By the mid-1970s, Ali had become a more devoted student of his faith and distanced himself from the separatist philosophy of Elijah Muhammad, the leader of the Nation of Islam. His spiritual growth and conversion to Sunni Islam in 1975 marked a significant turning point as he embraced a more inclusive and unifying approach. With Elijah Muhammad's passing, Ali had the opportunity to carve out his own path within Islam.

Ali's changing beliefs and attitude were evident in his statements during that time. He emphasized that he no longer harbored hatred towards white people and believed in a new phase of resurrection and unity. He expressed a humanitarian outlook and rejected the divisive teachings of Louis Farrakhan, the leader of the Nation of Islam, at a later period. Both supporters and critics recognized Ali's evolution as he transitioned from the narrow view of the Nation of Islam's early days to a broad universal view of Islam. Ali's willingness to evolve, embrace inclusion, and acknowledge his imperfections contributed to his humanitarian appeal. He recognized the need for change and growth, and his actions demonstrated a commitment to unity and justice. This, coupled with his charisma, eloquence, and ability to inspire people of all backgrounds, propelled him to a status of profound admiration and respect. Ali's journey from militancy to hope and his unwavering dedication to positively impacting the world are key factors in understanding his humanitarian legacy. Ali's heroic quality lies in his ability to acknowledge the context in which his involvement with the Nation of Islam occurred in the 1960s. While he initially embraced the separatist ideology of the organization, Ali's true beliefs did not align with the notion that whites were devils. He had personal relationships with white individuals he considered his closest friends and trusted associates.

In his heart, Ali recognized the importance of his role in advancing the cause of black Americans during that turbulent time, and the Nation of Islam provided a powerful platform for him to do so. However, as Ali's understanding and convictions evolved, he realized that hatred was not the path to progress. He would have distanced himself from the Nation of Islam much earlier if he hadn't feared for his safety, particularly considering the fate of Malcolm X, who was assassinated after leaving the organization. A significant turning point came in November 1974, following Ali's victory over George Foreman in Zaire. During an interview with white reporters, Nation of Islam security team members attempted to interrupt the conversation. Displaying his newfound assertiveness, Ali dismissed the security team and continued the interview, clearly expressing his frustration with the manipulative nature of the Nation of Islam's leadership. Ali's fear of the Nation of Islam and his acknowledgment that leaving the organization could potentially put his life at risk highlights the complex dynamics he faced. Despite these concerns, Ali held firm in his beliefs and understood that progress could only be achieved by working with people of all backgrounds. His evolution demonstrates a powerful transformation from militancy to inclusivity, as he recognizes the importance of unity and cooperation in advancing social justice. Ali's commitment to challenging unjust practices remained, but he shifted his approach, emphasizing the need for people of different backgrounds to collaborate towards shared goals.

Ali's regret over his initial alignment with Elijah Muhammad and the Nation of Islam, instead of Malcolm X is a significant aspect of his personal journey and growth. Ali recognized that Malcolm X had decided to pursue a more moderate approach to activism after his separation from the Nation of Islam. Ali deeply regretted not joining Malcolm X in pursuing solidarity and unity earlier. He acknowledged that Malcolm X's vision and insights were correct, and ultimately, Ali and others followed the path that Malcolm X had advocated for. When Ali received the news of Malcolm X's assassination, he was in Miami, focused on his training. Learning about the tragic event deeply affected Ali. He described it as a pity and a disgrace that Malcolm X had met such a fate, considering the validity of his ideas. Ali acknowledged that, in the end, they embraced the same principles and values that Malcolm X had espoused. This realization reflects Ali's growth and transformation, as he recognized the significance of unity and working towards common goals, which he might have started earlier had he aligned himself with Malcolm X. Ali's admiration for Malcolm X and his regret over not fully embracing his teachings highlight the profound impact that their friendship could have had on both their lives.

Indeed, in his latter years, Ali came to the opinion that one's character was most important, and he voiced deep remorse for his split with Malcolm X:

> Turning my back on Malcolm was one of the mistakes that I regret most in my life. I wish I'd told Malcolm I was sorry, that he was right about so many things. But he was killed before I got the chance. He was a visionary, ahead of us all. . . . Malcolm was the first to discover the truth that color doesn't make a man a devil. It is

the heart, soul, and mind that define a person. Malcolm X was a great thinker and an even greater friend. I might never have become a Muslim if it hadn't been for Malcolm. If I could go back and do it over again, I would never have turned my back on him.

Indeed, Muhammad Ali's ability to evolve, adapt, and learn from his life experiences was instrumental in his greatness. Both black and white individuals witnessed his growth, which further solidified his role as an ambassador for goodwill and advancing African Americans' cause. His symbolism transcended race, making him profoundly important in the history of black advancement. Ali understood the power of media and the importance of capturing attention. Even as a teenager, he sought to be the center of attention when cameras were present, pushing others aside. His natural charisma and charm made him a captivating subject for the camera. Photographers and artists alike recognized his unique qualities. He was described as a perfect subject, with his flawless features, perfectly proportioned physique, and timeless appearance that never changed.

The symbol of Ali went beyond mere popularity as a public figure. His physical and personal presence was larger than life, captivating people across different backgrounds and generations. He became an iconic figure, representing not only boxing prowess but also resilience, determination, and the ability to fight for justice and equality. Ali's ability to command attention and his magnetic presence contributed to his influence as a symbol and spokesperson for important social and cultural issues. He used his platform to advocate for change and inspire others to stand up against injustice. Muhammad Ali's fame and recognition extended far beyond the realm of sports. He was a global icon, known and revered by people from all corners of the world. No matter where he went, whether it was a hut in Africa, a village in Asia, or a marketplace in South America, people would recognize him and utter his name with a smile. His fame transcended borders, languages, and cultures. Even in remote parts of Africa and Asia, some individuals might not know the president of the United States but would undoubtedly know Muhammad Ali. He had an unparalleled level of international fame and popularity. Foreign heads of state would eagerly welcome and honor him. His global reach and recognition were evident in his ability to negotiate the release of American hostages in Iraq in 1991, showcasing his global influence and impact on a global scale.

Ali's extensive travels and experiences played a significant role in making him one of the most recognized individuals in the world. He boasted about his worldwide recognition in interviews, mentioning how people from Japan, China, Europe, Africa, Arab nations, South America, and beyond knew who he was. His larger-than-life persona and captivating presence left a lasting impression on people from diverse backgrounds and countries. The level of reverence and admiration Ali received was unparalleled. While there had been other champions in the past, none of them commanded the same level of global recognition and respect as Ali. He transcended the world of sports and became a symbol of inspiration, resilience, and social impact. To truly understand Ali's impact on African-American life, gathering insights and reflections from his contemporaries who covered his life and held relevant positions during his time is valuable. Their commentaries emphasize that Ali's significance extended far beyond his athletic achievements. He was a cultural and social icon who left an indelible mark on the world.

Indeed, the tragic events of September 11, 2001, had a profound impact on the world, and Muhammad Ali, despite his physical and verbal challenges due to Parkinson's disease, felt compelled to speak out and promote unity in the face of such devastation. As a Muslim and an American, he was uniquely positioned to bridge the gap between different faiths and cultures. Despite the difficulty he experienced in speaking full sentences, Ali made a national television appearance, expressing his hopes of bringing people together amidst the aftermath of the terrorist attacks. His physical condition, visibly affected by Parkinson's disease, and his emotional state, deeply shaken by the atrocities committed, further emphasized the sincerity and urgency of his message. Ali's presence and symbolic significance were instrumental in conveying the message of unity and understanding between Muslims and Christians. His personal journey, from his conversion to Islam to his advocacy for civil rights and humanitarian causes, made him influential in promoting peace and harmony. Ali's spirit and determination shone through despite his physical and verbal limitations, inspiring people to unite and find common ground. Ali's call for unity and his unique ability to resonate with people from different backgrounds and beliefs showcased his enduring humanitarian appeal during global shock and turmoil. He continued demonstrating his commitment to promoting understanding and harmony, leaving a lasting impact on the world, even in the face of personal challenges. As he had spoken out years before against racism and Vietnam, Ali said,

> "I'm a Muslim . . . People should know the real truth about Islam . . . I wouldn't be here representing Islam if it was really like the terrorists made it look . . . Islam is peace; against killing, murder; and the terrorists and the people doing it in the name of Islam are wrong; and if I had the chance I'd do something about it.

Indeed, Muhammad Ali was deeply troubled by the September 11 attacks and the negative portrayal of Islam. He recognized the danger of allowing terrorism to tarnish the reputation of an entire religion and its followers. Despite his declining health and verbal communication challenges, Ali remained steadfast in promoting unity and understanding among people of all faiths. Ali's experiences as a Muslim and his lifelong dedication to social justice and humanitarian causes fueled his determination to counteract the divisive narrative that emerged after the attacks. He understood the power of his voice and the influence he could wield, even in his diminished physical state. While his ability to speak full sentences may have been compromised by Parkinson's disease, Ali's unwavering resolve to unite people was undeterred. He emphasized that a few extremists' actions should not define an entire religion or its followers, and he encouraged dialogue, empathy, and mutual respect in the face of such adversity. By advocating for unity and understanding during a crisis, Muhammad Ali continued to exemplify the values of compassion, tolerance, and peace he had championed throughout his life. His efforts served as a reminder that even in the face of personal challenges, one can make a meaningful impact and inspire positive change in the world.

The recognition and honor bestowed upon Muhammad Ali, including receiving the Presidential Medal of Freedom from President George W. Bush in 2005, reflected his profound impact on people in America and worldwide. It was a significant moment highlighting Ali's transformation from a controversial figure who faced opposition for his stance on the Vietnam War to a revered and respected icon. President Bush's remarks during the award ceremony acknowledged the universal admiration for Ali, describing him as brave, compassionate, and charming. The fact that Ali, who had once been reviled by conservative Americans, was now being celebrated and honored by the establishment symbolized the extent of his influence and the change in public perception. Ali's role in the 1996 Atlanta Olympics, where he lit the torch in front of a global audience, further solidified his status as a beloved figure. President Bill Clinton's emotional reaction to Ali lighting the torch demonstrated Ali's deep impact on individuals and the power of his presence.

Towards the end of his life, Muhammad Ali had transcended racial divisions. He had evolved from emphasizing the beauty of being black and highlighting racial prejudices to becoming a unifying figure respected and admired by people of all backgrounds. Jerry Izenberg's observation that Ali was no longer seen primarily as a black man but as Muhammad Ali, a unique and universally recognized individual, speaks to the enduring legacy of his character and accomplishments. Muhammad Ali's journey from being a polarizing figure to a symbol of unity and inspiration is a testament to his personal growth, ability to connect with people from all walks of life, and unwavering commitment to principles of justice, compassion, and equality.

The impact of Muhammad Ali's life on African Americans was profound and far-reaching, reaching every corner of the country, from rural areas in the South to bustling cities. President Barack Obama's eulogy at Ali's funeral captured the essence of his influence, highlighting how Ali's journey represented the possibilities of a nation where a descendant of slaves could rise to become a global icon. Obama, himself a symbol of progress and change, acknowledged that Ali's example had inspired him as a young mixed-race individual with an unconventional name to believe in his potential, eventually becoming the President of the United States. Ali's legacy embodies America's spirit, reflecting his flamboyant, defiant persona and deep compassion and humanity. He challenged societal norms and fought against injustice, using his platform to advocate for civil rights, equality, and peace. Ali's life serves as a reminder of the audacity and resilience required to overcome adversity and make a lasting impact on the world. His legacy goes beyond his achievements in the boxing ring. Muhammad Ali's commitment to his principles, willingness to sacrifice for his beliefs, and ability to connect with people from all walks of life have solidified his place as an iconic figure in American history. He continues to inspire generations with his message of courage, perseverance, and social activism, leaving behind a legacy that celebrates both his individual greatness and his contribution to the progress of humanity.

His gift of words transformed African-American history and is mirrored in his intentions for leaving the world a better place: "I want them to put a few cups of love, one teaspoon of patience, one tablespoon of generosity, and one pint of kindness on my tombstone." Then he mixed it up, spread it over a lifetime, and offered it to everyone he met who deserved it."

Milton Keynes UK
Ingram Content Group UK Ltd.
UKHW020731220923
429186UK00015B/875

9 798223 394143